Oh Sh...Shunt!

The Brain Surgery and Fatih Transformation I Did Not See Coming

~

Ifedayo Greenway

Published by IG & MORE LLC

Virginia Beach, VA 23464

www.igandmore.com

ifegreenway@igandmore.com

Scripture quotations marked NLT are taken from the Holy Bible, New Living Translation Copyright © 1996, 2004, 2007, 2013, 2015 by Tyndale House Publishers Inc. Scripture quotations marked KJV are taken from the King James Version, Public domain. Scripture quotations marked MSG are taken from The Message Bible, Copyright © 1993, 1994, 1995, 1995, 1996, 2000, 2001, 2002 by Eugene H. Peterson. Scripture quotations are taken from The Holy Bible, New International Version® NIV® Copyright © 1973, 1978, 1984, 2011 by Biblica, Inc.™ Used by permission. All rights reserved worldwide

Printed in the United States of America

ISBN: 979-8-9994222-2-4

Ifedayo is available for speaking engagements, book signings, and workshops. Send your requests to ifegreenway@igandmore.com

Contents

Foreword

Written from the Heart of God

Daughter,

You may have wondered why. Why the pain, why the pressure, why the detour through discomfort when you were simply trying to live, serve, and show up well. You cried out from hospital beds, in the quiet of your room, in car rides, and in whispered prayers no one else heard. You weren't wrong to wonder. You weren't wrong to feel.

But I need you to know—*I was never far.*

I knew the diagnosis before the doctors did. I knew the medication wouldn't bring full relief. I knew the pressure would rise and your strength would falter. But I also knew *you would live.* I knew *you would heal.* I knew *you would write.*

Every tear you cried, I collected. Every question you asked, I heard. And every piece of your shattered understanding— I've been gently holding, reshaping, and using to build something greater than you imagined.

You see, I'm not just the God of healing—I'm the Author of your entire story. The One who knit you together is the One who knew how to keep you together. Nothing you walked through caught Me off guard. No medication, no diagnosis, no surgery, and certainly not the pressure.

It was never too much for Me.

And your children?

I was with them too.

When they sat quietly, trying to be strong for you—*I was their strength.*

When they carried fear in their eyes but hope in their hearts—*I was their peace.*

When they rose to the moment with courage, compassion, and maturity—*I was building character in them through it all.*

I comforted them when you couldn't. I whispered to their hearts when you were too weary to speak. I used this journey to deepen their faith, to show them that healing is not just something to hope for—it's something I *still do.* And in time, they too will look back and see how I fathered them while I was healing their mother.

You wanted quick relief. I was preparing a lasting testimony.

You wanted answers. I was giving you *authority.*

And now, as you turn these pages, know this:

I didn't just walk you through this—I carried you.

I didn't just let you survive this—I chose you to *speak* from it.

What the enemy thought would silence you, I've used to anoint you.

So write, daughter. Testify. Heal others as I have healed you.

Because I'm not done.

This is only the beginning.

—**Your Father, your Healer, your God.**

Author's Note

~

Before you dive in, let me share something about how this book is set up. You're about to walk with me through one of the most unexpected, life-altering journeys of my life. And I didn't want anything to break the flow of that story—not even the reflections that came out of it.

So instead of pausing after each chapter, I saved all the "*F It*" *Reflections* for the end of the book. Why? I just want us to journey together—uninterrupted, page by page—because this story isn't necessarily about being workbook material, it's about walking it out. Then, when you've finished the journey with me, you'll have a whole section of reflections waiting just for you. Think of it as our sit-down after the story's been told.

Now let me pause right here, because I know what you're thinking: "*F It? Did she really just say that?*" Yes, I did. And yes, it's a play on words. But stay with me. My "*FIt*" *Reflections* aren't about throwing my hands up and walking away—they're about **f**acing it, **f**eeling it, **f**aithing it, and finally finding my way through it. Each reflection gave me space to process what you're about to read through three lenses:

- **Fear Acknowledgement** – Naming the real and raw fears that show up when life turns upside down.

- **Faith Reflection** – A chance to lean into scripture and let God's truth speak louder than the trauma.

- **Final Resolution** – An invitation to anchor myself in hope and transformation as I kept moving forward.

So when you see *"F It,"* don't just think of it as a shrug and a surrender. Think of it as a bold declaration: *I'm going to face this thing, put my faith on it, and walk away with a resolution that pushes me into transformation.*

So read freely. Cry if you need to. Laugh when it comes. And when you're ready, circle back to the *"F It" Reflections* and let them guide you into your own kind of transformation.

Because sometimes the only thing left to say in an *"Oh Sh…Shunt"* moment is - *F It!*

Acknowledgments

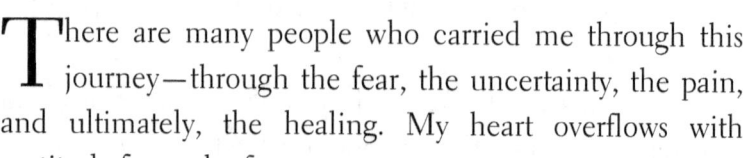

There are many people who carried me through this journey—through the fear, the uncertainty, the pain, and ultimately, the healing. My heart overflows with gratitude for each of you.

Mama – thank you for your unwavering love, strength, and prayers. You held space for me in the little red box, carrying the weight of every emotion that came with this season. You made the kind of sacrifices only a mother can make. You watched another chapter of my life unfold without asking, "Why, my baby girl?"—you simply trusted that God was doing something greater, and you kept warring for my purpose. Your presence—as my mom, my nurse, my prayer warrior, and my advocate—was nothing short of a lifeline.

Dad – you were adamant about talking with me on the phone as I drove to North Carolina, making sure I was safe on the road. You even extended the invitation to stay in your home, offering care and comfort through you and your wife. You called often, checking in to see how my healing journey was going. Your steadfast love and care reminded me of what it means to be a child always held in a father's heart. I love you for being my forever dad.

My Children, Rodney, Ahkei, Miya, and Nevaeh – words cannot capture how deeply grateful I am for each of you.

Rodney, you carried the weight of worry, hard conversations, and preparation for every possible outcome with grace and strength beyond your years. Ahkei, you were a strong caregiver, walking your siblings through moments of unspoken fear and teaching them how to hold on to their faith. Miya, I'm so grateful for our bond. Your courage and tenderness reminded me of the power of a child's faith. Nevaeh, your quiet presence, even in sleep, brought me comfort I didn't know I needed. You all reminded me why I could not give up, why I had to keep holding on, and why every healing moment mattered. Each of you held me in ways words can never fully express, and my heart will always carry the imprint of how you loved me through such a hard season.

Sandra – you were there from the very beginning, even before we knew surgery was the answer. You talked me through the hardest moments, accompanied me to appointments, and lifted us all in prayer. I can't thank you enough for being my friend and walking this road with me.

Angie and Stephanie – the memories of you doing my hair as if we were little girls again are priceless. Thank you for bringing laughter, comfort, and sisterhood into moments when I needed it most.

Dr. Keshia – the day you texted, *"I'll go to the doctor with you if you need me,"* I knew God had blessed me with a different kind of First Lady. Thank you for the encouraging texts, for reading medical notes with me, for guiding me through tough decisions, for showing up to pray, and for reminding me that giving up was never an option. I'll never forget the day you stood in church, looked me square in the face, and declared, *"You will have the surgery because God has more work for you to do."* Your confidence in my ability to rise and return to purpose was everything I needed.

The Mount at Chesapeake Intercessors – Min. Valencia and team, you prayed heaven down over me. Your faith, your fervor, and your intercession were felt in every moment of my healing journey.

Kenya – I don't even know where to begin. Thank you for nurturing and holding Miya, for sitting in my hospital room through some of the most private and hardest moments, and for speaking what my heart couldn't articulate through your random texts and voice notes. One moment in particular will stay with me forever—the day you brought me my hair in a bag. Whew. I didn't even realize you had saved it. When I saw it, I was overwhelmed with emotion. Cutting my hair had already been one of the hardest, most humbling moments of this journey, but realizing you had kept the remnants that fell into your hands after surgery revealed the depth of your care. You didn't let me face that loss alone. You carried it for me until I was strong enough to face it myself. Thank you doesn't even seem to scratch the surface or be enough for how you covered me.

Monique & Darlene – the group chats, the prayers, the love shared. You sat with me in church week after week, covering me in every moment of weakness. I knew you were praying, strategizing, and making sure my arms stayed lifted when I couldn't lift them myself. Your love and fervent prayers carried me through some of the weakest and most vulnerable moments of my faith. And Monique, even beyond the prayers, you held me accountable to write and tell this story. You wouldn't let me shrink back or stay silent—you pushed me to put words to my journey, and your guidance as my editor gave me the courage to release it.

Mrs. Marcia – thank you for showing up for me in ways both big and small. You checked on my scars when I couldn't bear to look in the mirror, shopped for me, called to make sure I was okay, and made sure I had a "nurse on call" at home. And then you searched high and low for that neck pillow—just so I could finally get some real rest. That kind of love and thoughtfulness stays with me. I love you deeply for that.

Cousin Kim – your sacrifice of being there almost every day, sitting with me, keeping the fridge full, and providing comfort in ways that words can't fully capture—thank you from the depths of my heart.

To all my family, friends, and those whose prayers lifted me even from afar: your love, support, and faith carried me through a season I could not have walked alone. I am endlessly grateful.

CHAPTER 1

When Life Hit Me in the Head

~~~

"This day could not be over fast enough."

That was the only thought keeping me tethered to my desk in my home office as the clock inched toward 5:00 PM. As a Financial Crimes Investigator, I had been glued to my computer for hours—combing through transactions, reviewing surveillance footage, conversing with law enforcement, and formulating meticulous details into comprehensive reports. My eyes burned. My brain felt like it was tired of thinking. But I needed to meet my daily case quota and keep up my pace with the demands of a job that had long since drained my joy. The stress level? An all-time high—way off the *healthy* charts and reading high levels of frequency on the *unhealthy* side of the meter. I was fed up with working cases and worn down with writing reports. I had to keep reminding myself that I was a child of God, because people were getting on my last nerve. I was one "Are you available?" message away from a full-blown cuss-out spree. There were times during the day when I would stare at my screen, my fingers hovering over the keyboard, trying to remember what I was even typing. I felt disconnected— like I was drifting through tasks I once took pride in, but now barely cared about. I was good at my job, but the passion?

Gone. My spirit had started to ache under the weight of performance. I often questioned if I was still doing what I was called to do—or if I was surviving out of habit, trapped in a "corporate world" rhythm that no longer made sense for who I was becoming.

Like so many days before, I had been working through yet another relentless headache. It had become my norm. I would wake up with it, grind through my day with it, and collapse into bed with that same dull, pulsing pain echoing through my skull that I woke up with. A couple of pain meds here and there, a prayer, and a push—and I made my way through the eight-hour shift.

But this day was different.

When I finally stood up to walk away from my computer, letting out a long, exhausted exhale, something happened. A sharp, almost electric jolt surged through the left side of my head. It wasn't just a headache—this was something else. Something deeper. Something...scary.

I froze and stood there for a minute.

"What was that?" I whispered, trying to steady my breathing. I had never felt anything like it.

I walked slowly to the bathroom, praying it was just a fleeting spasm. But then, staring at myself in the mirror, I noticed my vision was off. A shadowy blur drifted in my sight like an aggravating gnat refusing to leave. I blinked. Rubbed my eyes. Blinked again. It was still there. I stood there paralyzed for a few seconds, trying not to panic but unable to ignore the rising tide of worry that was creeping in. I wiped my face, as if cold water could rinse away the glaring floater in my eye. I turned my head from side to side, testing my vision, hoping—pleading—that whatever was happening would stop on its own. I even whispered out loud, *It's ok, you're ok…* trying to calm the storm brewing inside - trying to avoid what I didn't want to admit.

Something wasn't right.

It was too late to call the doctor that day. Offices were closed, and urgent care didn't feel like the right move—at least not yet. I stood there blinking, again and again, hoping that the little black floater would disappear, but it just lingered like an unwelcome guest in my vision. I prayed—quietly, urgently—that it was nothing major. *"Lord, please let this be nothing. Just stress. Just tiredness. Just…something small."* And to calm my racing thoughts, that's exactly what I told myself. *It's just stress.* That had become my default diagnosis for everything. Stress had become the blanket explanation for every ache, every pain, every moment my body cried out for rest. So I tucked the fear away in the folds of that familiar excuse and tried to convince myself that everything was fine.

I didn't want to think that this could be anything serious. I wasn't ready for "serious." Life had just hit me in the heart—and I was still reeling. I wasn't prepared for it to hit me in the head, too.

Just one month before this moment, I had hugged my only daughter—my Miya, my last child at home—and left her on a college campus in another state, five hours away from me. Driving away from her dorm felt like leaving a piece of my soul behind. That goodbye broke something in me.

We had become each other's best friends. Every night, we curled up in my bed like two little old ladies, watching game shows and guessing the answers out loud. We'd laugh until we cried and pause the TV to talk about life, school, or how ridiculous the contestants were. But beyond the laughs, we were each other's emotional anchor. We had walked through grief hand in hand—navigating the recent loss of her father, my ex-husband. We cried together. Held space for one another and reached for joy together in the middle of heartbreak. We didn't just grieve—we grieved *together*...and then slowly began to bounce back *together.*

So while leaving her on that campus was part of her natural "growing up" journey, it absolutely crushed my heart. The silence at home had been deafening ever since. I was adjusting to a new rhythm, a quieter house, and a void space that motherhood had once filled. Empty nest syndrome was kicking my butt, and my heart was still tender from the emotional blow of that transition.

Now here I was, standing in the bathroom, head pounding, vision altered, and fear whispering questions I didn't have the answers to. The possible truth was settling in slowly, rolling in through a back door I didn't see open: *Something might be wrong.*

The next morning, I called my optometrist as soon as the office opened. I wasn't sure who to call, so I figured I'd start there. As I described my symptoms, I noticed his tone shift. Concern crept into his voice, and he advised me—firmly— that I needed to see an ophthalmologist *right away.* He didn't leave it up to me to find one either. He scheduled the appointment for that same day.

I was nervous heading into the appointment, but I knew I didn't have a choice. I had to face whatever this was. As I signed in at the front desk, I prayed—silently, steadily—that it was nothing serious, or at least something simple and easily fixable.

The waiting room was quiet, except for the faint buzz of fluorescent lights and the sporadic conversations at the front desk as they signed in other patients. I scrolled aimlessly through my phone, trying to look unbothered, but my thumb kept freezing mid-scroll as my thoughts became more intrusive. My back ached from sitting so stiffly. Every time someone opened the door or came out to call a patient, my breath stopped—hoping and dreading that it would be my turn. I kept replaying my optometrist's voice in my head, trying to read between the lines of his concern. Was this caution… or was I dying? (Yup. I let my overthinking take me all the way there.) After about thirty minutes of simmering in that mental stew, my spiral was interrupted.

The nurse appeared, my patient file in hand, and called my name.

They began a series of eye tests—I never took so many eye pictures in my life: machines, scans, blinding lights. Then the doctor walked in. I watched closely as he pulled up strange-looking images on the screen—photos of my eyes that meant nothing to me, but meant something to him. He began dictating notes to his assistant using verbiage that I didn't understand, his eyes locked on the screen. I sat rigid, my nerves unraveling with every passing second. *Whew!* I silently yelled… *"Just tell me what is going on already."*

When he finally turned to speak to me, he began throwing out words like *papilledema, pseudo-tumor, swelling,* and *pressure.* My heart started racing. I was trying to track every syllable of the words that were coming out of his mouth and trying to make sense of what felt like a foreign language. The only thing I could truly grasp was this: the pain I'd felt the day before was the result of swelling behind my eyes— *especially* behind the left one. Seeing my panic rising, he gently tried to calm me down, emphasizing that "pseudo" means *false* He attempted to reel in my fear after using the word *tumor.* But that didn't exactly stop my mind from spiraling.

He went on to tell me that although he was pretty certain about what was wrong, he couldn't fully diagnose me. He explained that the swelling behind my eyes was serious, but not something he could conclusively label because it was ultimately a head issue. He would need to refer me to a "neuro-something-or-another"—his words were blurring together at that point—for more testing and evaluation.

Needless to say, I left that office with more questions than I had walked in with. The most blaring one— *What is wrong with me?*

I went home, prayed, and had a few too many in-depth conversations with Dr. Google. (And let's be honest—Dr. Google will have you thinking you have two weeks to live.) Every article, every medical term, every forum post added more anxiety to my already overloaded mind. While in the office, I had snapped a photo of the images the doctor had pulled up on the screen, so I was now searching for similar pictures online—anything that might explain things a little better. I was hoping the referral process would take some time—that maybe I'd have a few days to exhale, to process, and to finish diagnosing myself.

But just a couple of days later, my phone rang.

"Ms. Greenway? We need to schedule you for a spinal tap."

And just like that…life was about to change.

It turns out, life wasn't done swinging at me…and this time, it came straight for my head.

CHAPTER 2

Fifty Seven: Does Pressure Really Bust Pipes?

~

"We have you scheduled for October 16th at 11:30."

I scribbled the date and time onto a notepad like it was just another appointment—like I was jotting down a meeting or a routine dentist visit. But when I went to add it to my iCal, my hand trembled slightly as I typed in the deets.

Spinal tap.

Two words I never imagined would be tied to my name in a medical chart. The clinical phrase felt cold, almost detached—but everything in me was on high alert. Behind my calm, "Okay, thank you," was a swirl of fear, confusion, and the creeping realization that this was real.

Something was happening inside me that couldn't be ignored or explained away as stress anymore. This wasn't just pressure in my life—it was pressure in my head. Building. Blurring. Demanding to be investigated.

And just like that—with one phone call and a time stamp—the next chapter of my story had officially begun. The chapter where the pressure didn't just threaten to burst my life open—it surged with urgency, exposing every hidden crack and blockage that hindered its flow.

Pressure busts pipes is one of those phrases people toss around when life gets too heavy—when the weight becomes unbearable and something finally gives. I'd heard it before, but now I was about to live it. Head first.

I was about to find out—firsthand—whether pressure breaks… or builds.

I was nervous—really nervous. I didn't know what to expect. Sure, I'd given birth before (I have three children) and experienced an epidural, which is somewhat similar in procedure. Still, something about having a big ol' needle inserted into my back for this reason hit different. And honestly, I still didn't fully understand how a spinal tap was connected to whatever was going on in my head.

A little more Google research and I learned, a spinal tap— also called a lumbar puncture—is a procedure used to collect cerebrospinal fluid (CSF) from the spinal canal. This fluid surrounds the brain and spinal cord, and analyzing it helps doctors diagnose conditions that affect the brain and central nervous system.

A few days passed between the scheduling and the day of the appointment. I braced myself for what felt like a daunting medical moment. I'd been told the whole process would only take a couple of hours, so I prepared accordingly. My best friend, Sandra, agreed to come with me since someone needed to accompany me and drive me home. She arrived at my house just in time to get us there an hour early. We arrived at the outpatient facility in the happiest of moods. Despite the circumstances, our spirits were high. Sandra had prayed with me before we left, and on the drive over, we were in our normal friendship element —laughing at our stupid jokes, judging people's driving skills, and even planning what we'd grab for lunch once it was all over.

But what was supposed to be a two-hour appointment quickly turned into an all-day ordeal: CT (Computed Tomography) scans, Magnetic Resonance Venography (MRV) imaging, bloodwork, and long stretches of waiting. For context, an MRV is a non-invasive imaging technique that uses magnetic fields and radio waves to produce detailed pictures of the veins in the brain. It's often used to detect issues with venous blood flow, like clots or structural abnormalities.

We were doing our best to be patient. I hadn't eaten all day because I was told to fast in preparation for the anesthesia. Sandra, being the ride-or-die friend she is, tried her best not to act like she was hungry—but I knew that chick was starving just like I was. She didn't want me to have any thoughts of food. We kept joking around, trying to lighten the mood while we waited, but truthfully, after about two hours, I was unraveling inside, and she was doing her best to remain my solid emotional support.

They were having trouble getting my IV started—multiple attempts, multiple sticks—and eventually, they had to call in a specialist to get the needle in. That alone made me feel like this whole thing was already too much.

I lay there in a thin hospital gown, in a cold room that didn't offer much comfort, trying to quiet the mental noise. I kept thinking, *This will all be worth it. This has to lead to answers. This has to prove that everything is okay...* But then came the creeping question that I couldn't shake: What if there is something seriously wrong with me?

Once they finally took me back for the procedure, everything moved in a blur. I remember looking around the room—bright lights overhead, big screens near the procedure table, medical staff moving quickly, speaking in clipped, clinical tones. I heard them confirming the procedure and discussing the dosage of Fentanyl they were about to inject into my IV, each voice layering on top of the other like background noise in a scene I wasn't sure I wanted to be in.

"Fentanyl?" I asked, my voice cracking with concern. The only thing I knew about that drug was what I had seen on the news or in TV shows—people dying from it. My heart raced. Wasn't that the stuff taking people out? The nurse paused and reassured me, gently but firmly, that this was not that. The medication was safe here, carefully controlled in this environment, and nothing like the street version that was making headlines. I nodded, but the knot in my stomach tightened.

As one of the nurses gently placed a warm blanket over me, I caught her eye and whispered, "I'm scared." That moment felt like my last bit of emotional honesty. The nurse didn't say much—she just nodded with a reassurance that was so profound, it felt like God Himself was telling me I'd be okay. So, I relaxed, yielded to the medicine that had been injected in my veins, and drifted off.

And when I woke up, I was suddenly in a full-on relationship with a number I never invited into my life. No warning, no buildup, no foreplay—just smack dab in the middle of an unexpected entanglement with an unassuming integer: 57.

I learned that my intracranial pressure was 57.

Normal is somewhere between six and twelve. That means my number was more than four times the normal maximum. Fifty. Seven.

I couldn't process what that number meant for my life—only that it didn't sound survivable. My ears kept ringing with it. 57. Fifty-seven. I kept repeating it like I was trying to convince myself it wasn't real. But it was. And it was in my head—literally. The same head that had been throbbing nonstop, the same eyes that had started blurring and dimming, the same body that felt like it was holding its breath under the weight of something I couldn't see.

Was my head about to explode?

How was I even alive?

It felt like they'd just told me my brain was drowning in silence. I imagined pressure building like steam in a locked pot—no whistle, no release valve, no warning system except pain—just mounting force, pushing against the inside of my skull, threatening to blow. I wasn't sure if I should thank God (I mean, surely I should)…panic or both.

My diagnosis: Idiopathic Intracranial Hypertension.

Which is a clinical way of saying, "Your pressure is way too dang high."

High intracranial pressure—also called intracranial hypertension—means there's increased pressure inside the skull. It's not just uncomfortable; it's dangerous. If untreated, it can lead to irreversible vision problems, brain damage, or even death.

It can be caused by several things—head injuries, brain tumors, or an excess of cerebrospinal fluid. In my case, it was that last one. The fluid around my brain wasn't draining like it was supposed to. It was just sitting there… chilling… wreaking all kinds of pressure havoc.

Why was it doing that? The doctors had no idea. That's why they call it Idiopathic—meaning, "we don't know the cause."

And the symptoms?

Headaches that refused to let go.

Vision changes that showed up uninvited.

Nausea. Vomiting. Dizziness.

Mental fog. Confusion.

And fear—so much fear.

I was lying there, post-procedure, in the recovery room, wrapped in a blanket, trying to hold on to just one clear thought: What does 57 as a pressure point mean for me?

The nurse had mentioned it casually—but her tone carried weight. As she went over the possible diagnoses, she said, "If it's what we suspect, there are only two medications we typically use." Then she added, almost like a warning, "Most people struggle with both. The side effects can be... life-altering."

At the time, I tucked that information away, not ready to unpack it. After a full day in the hospital—CT scans, blood work, MRVs, the spinal tap, the waiting—I was finally released.

Still drowsy from the anesthesia, I climbed into Sandra's car. She and I are usually very authentic in our conversations, but neither of us brought up the insurmountable number. 57. We danced around it. Instead, we tossed around food ideas, trying to land somewhere between comfort and convenience. When we got to my house, she made sure I was tucked into bed before heading back out to grab dinner.

She stayed the night—to make sure I was okay. I love her for being the friend she is.

I remember her quietly stepping into my bedroom the next morning to tell me she was heading out. I nodded, still floating somewhere between gratitude and exhaustion.

Later that day, my phone rang right as I had allowed myself to forget about the medical drama and enjoy a meal. It was the doctor, with an urgent and quick call.

"We need to start you on medication right away," he said.

I paused, internally saying, "I know you lyin.'"

"You mean the same medication the nurse said makes people feel like everything else except normal?"

Silence. Then: "Yes... that one."

I exhaled and cried.

Not a dramatic, chest-heaving cry—just that quiet kind of sob that slips out when you realize: this is real now. I am not ok. I knew I was in for a long ride as we began the journey of trying to lower my intracranial pressure.

In the days to follow, 57 rang in my mind nonstop - constantly ricocheting off of every positive thought that I tried to muster up. Because my number had been so high, they started me on a fairly aggressive dosage. And it didn't take long to understand precisely why the nurse had said what she said.

Almost immediately, the side effects rolled in like a wave. I was constantly tired, but not the kind of fatigued a nap could fix. My hands and feet tingled nonstop—like pins and needles that never eased up. I was nauseous, drowsy, and foggy… like I was walking through my life underwater.

And on top of that, the headaches hadn't let up. The pressure in my head still pulsed, and my vision was paying the price.

After a few weeks of trying to live, work, and function through all of that, I finally reached out to my doctor and asked the question I had been holding in:

"Is there anything else we can try?"

I wasn't trying to be difficult. I was trying to be functional.

Yes, the medication was doing something—but it was also doing too much. I couldn't tell what was worse: the symptoms of the condition or the side effects of the treatment. Somewhere in the middle of that chaos, I was still expected to show up to work, answer texts, be a mom, GMa, life-coach, book coach, and ministry leader, and to do it all like I wasn't falling apart.

Only my close family and a few trusted friends knew what I was going through. I hadn't shared anything publicly—no social media posts, no hints online that something was wrong. So most people still expected that Dayo—the strong one, the dependable one, the "she's gonna be fine" version—to show up.

But truthfully, I was living in a space between pressure and pills and navigating a body that no longer felt like mine. Carrying a brain that wouldn't stop reminding me: something is off.

I was taking these life-altering pills three times a day. At one point, I called the doctor's office again and asked if we could either lower the current dosage or try the second medication. Remember, there were only two options for this diagnosis. After I explained my side effects—fatigue, tingling, nausea, confusion—I remember the nurse saying casually, "Yeah, it's a really powerful drug."

There was a part of me that wanted to scream. They knew it would make me feel like this… and they gave it to me anyway. But I also understood—we didn't have many choices. They were doing what had to be done, and so was I.

We tried the second medication, but my symptoms didn't improve at all. The headaches grew more intense, and even the simplest daily tasks felt like climbing uphill with bricks strapped to my back.

So, back to the first one we went—this time on a lower dose. I decided to grit my teeth and learn how to live with the side effects. By then, I had done enough of my research to know that if medication didn't work, the next stop would be surgery.

Things got worse before they got better.

The doctors spent weeks adjusting my dosages, trying to find that elusive *sweet spot.* At one point, they added even more medications—a pill specifically for migraines, and a regular injection in my leg for daily headaches.

The medication saga, the symptoms, the side effects… they all began to wear me down.

Living alone, I became afraid. What if something happened while I was by myself? What if the side effects knocked me out and no one was there to help? The anxiety of *what if* started to weigh just as heavily as the pressure in my head. So, I packed a bag and drove five hours to my mama's house. I needed more than just supervision—I needed comfort, covering, and care.

I stayed for two weeks while starting the next round of medication, just to make sure someone could keep an eye on me in case things went left. And one thing about my mama—she's a die-hard praying woman—a bona fide intercessor. So, while I was there, she didn't just offer support; she covered me in a way only a mother could. She anointed my head and body with oil and whispered healing prayers that felt like balm to my soul. She walked the floors in the middle of the night calling on God by name, speaking life over my body, peace over my mind, and strength into my spirit.

In that house, I wasn't just watched—I was warred for.

Eventually, it all became too much to carry while trying to work. My doctor put me on medical leave so I could focus solely on healing and managing the storm inside my body.

Almost two months passed.

Then came the next marker in this journey: the second spinal tap. The doctors needed to check if the chaos of all these meds had done anything—had my pressure dropped enough to safely send me back to work?

I scheduled the outpatient procedure. My hopes were just as high as my intracranial pressure. I had done the hard work— five months of treatment, medication, rest, and relentless prayer. Surely something had shifted.

It was time to find out:

Had the pressure busted my pipes… or had it yielded to me relentlessly fighting back?

CHAPTER 3

Oh Sh...Shunt!

～～

"Rodney, did the doctor talk to you already?"

"Yes, Ma."

"What did he say?"

He heard me but turned his head, eyes shifting to his phone—not to ignore me, but to pretend that my question was rhetorical so that he could respectfully avoid answering.

"Rodney," I called his name again, this time in a quiet, urgent whisper. "What did he say?"

"Ma, I heard you the first time," he said, barely above a whisper. "I didn't answer... because it's not good."

Nothing else needed to be said.

Tears welled in my eyes and slipped down my cheeks without permission. The sedation still lingered in my body—I was suspended between alert and numb, like I was waking up into a nightmare I didn't sign up for.

Rodney, my oldest son, had come with me for the second spinal tap procedure, which was in February 2025, five months after the first one. I hadn't wanted to go through another invasive test, but I agreed to this one—hoping, praying that it would finally bring clarity. That it would bring good news. That it would be the gas I needed to accelerate and turn the healing corner.

I squeezed his hand, letting my tears speak the words I couldn't bring myself to say. And without hearing a single word from the doctor myself, I knew exactly what my son was not saying.

A few seconds into the heavy silence, the doctor walked into my recovery room.

"Ms. Greenway," his voice flat and clinical, like he wasn't about to alter the course of my entire life. "Your pressure is still very high. I'm referring you to a neurosurgeon… you'll need a shunt placed in your brain."

He went on to explain that this time, my intracranial pressure was reading greater than 57. "What's the number?" I asked. He said, I'm not even sure because the machine only goes to 57 (no one is expected to be that high), after that, it just shows greater than."

Oh sh…shunt!

I had heard the word shunt before. I didn't know much, but what I did know was enough to terrify me. My brain. Surgery. Something permanent. Something implanted. They want to go inside my brain?

I didn't say anything at first. I just lay there, staring at the ceiling, trying to slow the swirl of panic forming in my chest.

I remember asking the doctor, "Are you sure?"

He nodded. "It's the best way to relieve the pressure long term. Medication isn't giving us the results we need." He was calm. Methodical. It was almost like he was recommending a flu shot. But what he was suggesting was far from a simple remedy. I turned to Rodney. I could see the worry behind his eyes, the silent calculations happening in his head. I was his mother, but in that moment, I felt like a child again — vulnerable, scared, looking for someone to tell me everything would be okay. When it was time, I was released, and my son took me home.

He did his best to care for me, knowing that the news I'd just received was nothing short of a medical gut punch. I was still groggy — drifting in and out from another dose of fentanyl — when I smelled the food he made for dinner. Baked chicken with rice and gravy. Asparagus on the side. He served it quietly, gently. Waiting on me hand and foot, like he was trying to offer comfort where words couldn't reach. Cooking has always been his love language.

That night, I rested — but not deeply. My body was still sedated, but my mind was starting to wake up to the weight of it all. Being the oldest of my three kids. He also had the difficult task of keeping his brother, sister, and other family members informed about the doctor's diagnosis. I could hear the conversations happening around me, voices hushed but heavy, lingering just outside the room. Nobody brought the complicated conversation to me right away, and I wasn't rushing to join any table talk sessions around the daunting recommendations of my doctor. Either way, the silence settled between us like a fragile truce. Everyone is trying to be strong. Everyone is trying to be careful. But the truth was loud—louder than any words we could have spoken.

My worst fears and negative expectations were being materialized. Brain surgery had made a grand entrance and ushered itself to the head of the treatment table.

I waited anxiously to get a call from the neurosurgeon's office. I knew that once they received the referral, they'd contact me to schedule my consultation. I found myself trapped in a strange emotional limbo, torn between contradictory desires. Part of me said, "Hurry up and call!" While the other half whispered, "Please don't call at all."

But finally, the phone rang.

My appointment was scheduled for March 4, 2025—three weeks after my second spinal tap. A small fragment of my heart clung to the hope that maybe this surgery talk wasn't as serious as it sounded. If it were truly urgent, wouldn't they have rushed to see me right away? Or maybe I was just desperate to find hope in anything.

Coincidentally, my initial consultation with the neurosurgeon was scheduled on the same day I was set to see my neurologist for a follow-up. The neurologist appointment was in the morning, and the neurosurgeon's appointment was in the afternoon. I crafted a whole plan in my *broken* head: go to both appointments and plead—beg—that we give the medication more time to work. I was even willing to be put on the absolute highest dosage, regardless of the side effects.

Somewhere in my remedy journey, one of the doctors had casually mentioned that losing a little weight might help bring my pressure down (even though gaining weight wasn't the cause of my condition). So, I took that to heart, too. Although I am an emotional eater and felt like I needed food to comfort me, I had mentally committed to skipping meals, fasting if I had to. Hell, I was ready to forgo eating altogether if it meant taking surgery off the table. I was prepared to do whatever it took. Anything. I just needed more time. More time to pray. More time to try. More time to fix myself. Because surgery felt like the end of something I wasn't ready to release. It wasn't just about avoiding the scalpel—it was about feeling like I still had a say. Like I still had control. But deep down, I could feel that grip loosening. I was reluctantly and grudgingly releasing my sense of control, my ability to choose how this healing would happen, my faith in my resilience.

March 4th arrived, and I was like a soldier with marching orders—ready to implement my self-constructed plan. My daughter, Miya, was home from college on Spring Break, and I felt good about having what I thought was a ride-or-die soldier with me to carry out the mission.

That morning, I went to my neurologist. When he walked into the room, I went in hard, laying out the list of things I was willing to do if they would give me more time. I was determined, desperate even. He wasn't on board at first. He kept pointing back to how high my pressure had been and made it very clear that putting off surgery would not be his recommendation.

Then finally, he caved—with a caveat. He agreed to give me three months to do everything possible to get that daunting *greater than 57* pressure down. The stipulations were clear:

If anything about my symptoms changed, the deal was off. If the neurosurgeon felt differently, the surgeon's recommendation would override everything. Whew. When I left his office, I was ecstatic and hopeful. It felt like the first victory in all of this. I had three months to prove I could get better, that I didn't need brain surgery. Miya hadn't gone with me to the first appointment, but when I got home, I shared the news with her and fully expected her to be just as excited as I was.

But by the afternoon, things had shifted. Miya had spoken to her brothers and they gave her a new set of marching orders for the second appointment with the neurosurgeon. On the car ride there, she made it clear that she—on behalf of her siblings—had some questions for the surgeon.

We arrived at the neurosurgeon's office, checked in, and were quickly taken to a consultation room. Miya had her iPad open with documented questions to make sure she didn't miss anything—she had to report back to her brothers. When the neurosurgeon came in, I felt a glimmer of hope. Not just because he was easy on the eyes (whew, chile... let me stop), but because his smile was warm and his demeanor felt genuinely agreeable. We had a good chance of getting him on board with the three-month plan. He thoroughly explained what the surgery would entail and explained that the shunt would reroute the excess cerebrospinal fluid from my brain to my abdomen, through a thin tube placed under the skin. It sounded robotic. Mechanical. Foreign. My mind heard, *we're going to cut into your head and hope for the best.* He even brought in a shunt for me to see and physically touch. After going through all the details, he asked, "What questions can I answer for you?" Miya didn't wait. "I'll go first," she said, before I could even open my mouth. Her first question came from a deep place of fear, undoubtedly tied to the recent loss of her father: "Am I going to lose my mommy?" Hearing those words out loud shattered me. I could hardly fathom the weight pressing on her young heart, grappling with the terrifying thought of losing the one parent she had left, especially after witnessing firsthand the toll her father's death had already taken on her. She was far too young to be carrying the burden of such a question. And yet, I knew she needed to ask it—for her emotional grounding and sense of security. The surgeon gently assured her that he wouldn't let anything happen to me—not in a way that suggested he was God, but with a quiet confidence that made it clear he knew God would be guiding his hands. Then, Miya shifted into full business mode, her little shoulders straightening as if she were preparing for a boardroom meeting rather than a hospital conversation.

"The other doctor told Mommy she could wait three more months. Is waiting helping her or hurting her?"

"Hurting her," he said without hesitation. She documented his response.

After a few more questions—mostly hers—she turned to me and said, "Mommy, you're having the surgery."

I wanted to scream, Wait, whose side are you on?! We came in here together with a plan—two true soldiers—and she had left me on the battlefield fighting alone.

I was proud of her maturity in that moment, but I was also low-key mad that she had aborted our mission. When it was all over, the doctor directed us to the scheduler's office. It was all happening too fast. She had an opening just three weeks later. Somehow, I knew I needed to accept it. As she was scheduling, I saw Miya lift her iPad to her face, and soon I could hear soft sobs behind its shield. That was all it took for me to break down, too. I sat there trying to work through all the logistics while crying and trying to console her—both of us were emotional wrecks by that time. Even the scheduler looked like she was struggling not to cry. I wish I could fully articulate the emotional narrative of that moment—the weight of fear, the ache of uncertainty, the tenderness between a mother and daughter who were both trying to be strong for each other but falling apart at the same time. Our tears said everything words could not.

Miya and I grabbed hands, walked out, and just like that, my brain surgery was scheduled for March 20th, 2025. It was no longer just a possibility. It was a date. A decision. A doorway we had no choice but to walk through—together.

CHAPTER 4

Pre-op Panic & Prayers

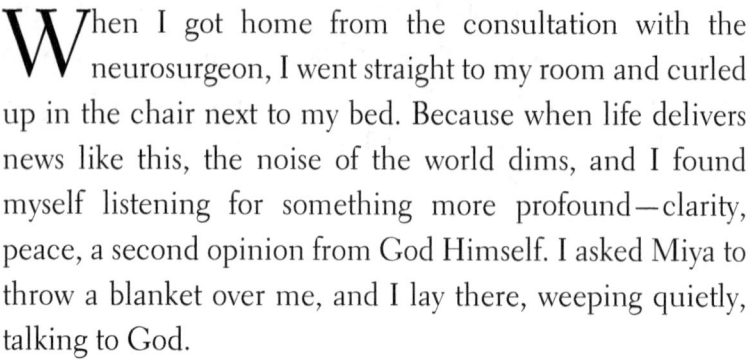

When I got home from the consultation with the neurosurgeon, I went straight to my room and curled up in the chair next to my bed. Because when life delivers news like this, the noise of the world dims, and I found myself listening for something more profound—clarity, peace, a second opinion from God Himself. I asked Miya to throw a blanket over me, and I lay there, weeping quietly, talking to God.

"God, I need You to explain this one. I'm out of strength. I don't have another fight in me unless You give it to me."

I trusted Him. I did. But I couldn't help but ask the quiet question echoing in the back of my mind: *Why would You let me go through all of this—the pills, the side effects, the isolation, the anxiety—to end up here?*

Wasn't I obedient? Wasn't I faithful? I took the meds. I went to the appointments. I plowed through the headaches and still managed to whisper prayers between the pain. But now… surgery?

It felt like all the hell I went through with the medication hadn't bought me any relief—it had just bought me a front row seat to the next hard thing. And I didn't want to admit it, but there was a part of me that felt forgotten. Not forsaken—I didn't believe He had abandoned me. But I wondered if I had slipped through the cracks—if this particular kind of suffering had snuck past His hand.

I knew better spiritually, but emotionally? I was so freaking raw.

While I lay there, my phone rang twice. The first time, it was a dear friend calling to make sure I was home so she could bring over wine and dinner—she wasn't about to let me wallow too long. After I hung up with her, I tried to put the phone on "Do Not Disturb," but another call came in before I could.

"Ms. Greenway, this is Joseph. Do you have a moment?"

I wiped my tears, sat up in the chair, and braced myself. This was the recruiter for a job I'd been interviewing for while juggling everything else in my life. I know it sounds wild, with everything I was going through and already being out on medical leave, but I had applied for a new job. I couldn't go back to the mundane stressors of the one I had been working on for the last twelve years…. and somehow, I had found the strength to dress up the top half of my body and show up mentally for four interviews.

"Yes," I replied.

He gave me the usual *thank you for your interest* spiel, and just as I thought he was about to let me down gently, he offered me the position I'd been praying for. Not only the job, but a salary and benefits package beyond what I'd asked for. And, as if this was some divine alignment, he offered a start date that gave me almost four weeks to recover from surgery.

It was one of those surreal, spiritual moments. I felt like God had met me in one of my darkest places and reminded me that He was still there. At least I had something to look forward to after this nightmare was over. Although graced with this glimpse of hope, I was still spiraling. For the next few days, I sat with the word *shunt* like it was a stranger; like we were being introduced to each other for some forced marriage. I Googled. I overthought. I prayed a little and panicked a lot. By this point, my immediate family, close friends, and spiritual leaders knew I was preparing for this pivotal moment—but I hadn't told many others. How do you casually explain that doctors want to put a tube in your brain? I was still trying to wrap my head around it (literally).

I had three weeks between the surgeon saying, "We need to do this," and the day I would be wheeled into the operating room. That's 21 days to prepare. I tried to get my house in order, tie up loose ends at work, smile at people who didn't know my world was caving in—but inside, I was contending with what felt like uncontrollable fear and anxiety.

There's something different about preparing for a surgery on my brain. It's not a knee, a kidney, or a gallbladder.

It's my mind.

My memories.

My creativity.

My thoughts.

My dreams.

My identity.

Just over a week before surgery, I stood in front of the mirror with a comb in one hand and anguish in the other. I was preparing to take my braids out and wash my hair. As I looked at the strands, the curls, the crown I'd nurtured and styled with care, it hit me: I was about to lose it. Just about half of it. Shaved. Violated. Cut into. Accessed like a map they needed to read.

I crumbled on the inside.

And *that* was the day I grieved my hair.

One of the most frustrating things was trying to explain why this part of the journey was so hard. Whenever I expressed my sadness at having my head shaved I got responses like, "It's just hair. It'll grow back," or "You need to listen to the song, *I Am Not My Hair* by India Arie." Their intentions were good, but no one seemed to understand the depth of violation I felt. My hair wasn't just strands—it held memories. It had been twisted, wrapped, mostly braided, and pulled back into ponytails. It had been oiled by loving hands, complimented in passing, and marveled at in mirrors. Now, it would be removed to save my life.

My hair was a part of my beauty, yet it wasn't vanity I was feeling—it was mourning.

In many Black cultures, hair is a sacred thread woven into identity, femininity, and resilience. It's how we tell our stories before we speak. We wear our hair in styles we are proud of—locs, braids, twist-outs, silk presses, afros, protective styles, short cuts, even bald heads. For some women, a shaved head is a bold and beautiful choice. But there is a profound difference between choosing to accent your beauty in a way that reflects your self-expression and having someone take clippers to your head, shaving away a part of you with no regard for what it means—or what it will look like afterward.

Losing my hair wasn't a cosmetic shift. It was a grieving. The loss before the healing even began. As I processed through this grief moment, something else was beginning to rise - my frustration with God. That night, I argued with Him. Loudly.

Wasn't this enough?

Hadn't I already lost enough pieces of myself in this journey—my peace, my strength, my sense of control, my ability to pretend I was okay? Hadn't I trusted Him when the medication failed? When the spinal taps were too much? When the pressure numbers read off the charts like my head was housing a storm?

I sobbed into my pillow, whispering words I thought *good* Christians weren't supposed to say:

GODDDD!!!!..."*Take this thorn, Jesus. Please. I've carried it long enough.*"

But He didn't. Not that night.

Instead, I lay there with my hair still on my head, my heart cracked open, and an upcoming appointment straight to the operating room (OR). The reality of heading into brain surgery pushed me to confront something even deeper than losing my hair: *my mortality.* What if something goes wrong? What if I don't wake up? What if I wake up but I'm not fully me—if I lose my mind, my memories, my voice? I fought hard to stay spiritually grounded and think positive thoughts, but the fear was real. I remember thinking, *What will my children do if the doctors come out of that OR and tell them, "She didn't make it?"* I went through the mental torture of imagining each one of their responses.

Somewhere in the middle of that dark imagining, my thoughts turned inward. A friend who was also a grief therapist once told me, "People die the way they live." I recalled that statement during a moment when I was deeply reflecting on my life and death—wondering if the way I had been living would be something I'd be proud to die from... or something I'd regret. It stopped me. Made me take an honest inventory. There were areas of my life I was proud of—my resilience, my faith, my ability to show up for others—but when it came to relationships, I wasn't proud at all. I had spent years navigating relationships like obstacle courses—trying to earn love, prove my worth, settle just to be chosen. I tolerated the revolving door of rejection, all while craving stability and connection.

And I realized:

If I were to die in that OR, I didn't want to leave this world the same way I had moved through it—uncertain of my value and surrounded by people who couldn't or would never see it either.

So I made a choice. I cleaned up my circle.

I became very intentional about who I wanted at the hospital when I went in. I wanted to be covered in genuine love. And as I thought about who I needed most, my heart couldn't help but circle back to my dad. I know without a doubt that my dad loves me in the most unadulterated way, but the truth is our relationship has had its share of strain. Nothing broken beyond repair, but things we were intentionally working through—committing to talk more, spend more time together, and show up better for each other. If I'm honest, there were times when I felt like I was pushing harder for the relationship than he was, and I think that's part of what slowed me down from telling him about the surgery right away. Deep down, I wanted my daddy—the tall, strong man who, in my eyes, could fix anything—to be there and tell me that everything was going to be okay. We played phone tag for a couple of days, and when I finally reached him and told him my surgery date, he let me know he was already scheduled to be traveling at that time. I understood. I wasn't angry, and I didn't fault him—it was a surprise surgery date for all of us, and life has its conflicts. But the little girl in me was still sad at the thought of my dad not being there. No matter how grown you are, there are moments when you just want your father's presence.

Right at one week before surgery, I had to go to the hospital for some additional pre-op tests. As I sat there, my mind and emotions heavy, I suddenly remembered that the chapel at the hospital was named after my Bishop. Something in me knew I needed to find it. When I walked in and saw "Bishop Kim Walter Brown & Elder Valerie K. Brown Interfaith Chapel," with their pictures on the wall, peace surrounded me. I sat, cried, and prayed—not idolizing my leaders, but simply grateful that God, in His kindness, reminded me I was still covered. My dad couldn't be there, but my spiritual father's presence—in that very hospital—was a reassurance that I was not alone.

I snapped a picture of me standing in front of the sign and picture on the wall, and texted Bishop:

"Good morning Bishop! I'm scheduled to have brain surgery at Chesapeake Regional next week. I'm a little bummed about my dad not being able to be with me, but at my pre-op appointment today, God reminded me that my spiritual

father has a presence in the hospital and that I am in fact covered! I'm grateful for your reach. Love you."

He called me right away, reassured me about my neurosurgeon, and promised he'd be praying for me. It was just another reminder of how God was weaving His presence into every intricate detail of this season. Nobody could ever take the place of my Dad, but I do appreciate the way God used that moment to make me even more sure of my village of love. Even when fear and disappointment tried to strip me bare, He reminded me that my heavenly Father had me wrapped in His protection. And there, standing in the gap on earth, was my spiritual father—covering me in prayer and presence. Together they echoed the same truth in different ways: *"You're still covered—in more ways than one."*

The other beautiful—and painful—thing was, I didn't have to remove anyone from my life or circle that wasn't supposed to be there. They removed themselves. Their silence, their absence, their lack of support told me everything I needed to know. And for once in my life, I didn't chase after them. I let them go. Only holding close to me those that I knew loved me to life - including my daddy.

What I know for sure is, the ones who were meant to walk with me? *They showed up.* In presence. In prayer. In power. One of the most beautiful manifestations of having a village that truly loved me came when I needed it the most. I was exhausted, emotionally tender, doing all the last-minute pre-op tests, trying to stay upright under the weight of it all—

when my middle child, Ahkei, dropped this in our family group chat:

Good morning family,

Everyone should be fasting in some way this week. Mom originally said 24–48 hours before the day, but by the time we do it on Tuesday or Wednesday, I believe we should dedicate our week to preparing for it.

This isn't about you being the most spiritual person. This isn't about sacrifice = good results. This is solely about us being in alignment, which is essentially what fasting is for: a reset, a listening tool, and a heart cleanser.

Fasting isn't only about food, but what would legit be a sacrifice for you to give up for the next 5 days? It could be social media until 6 pm. It could be no juice for the whole week. It could be no sweets. For Rodney, it could even mean no gaming. Although it's not about choosing the hardest thing, it's not about choosing the easiest thing either.

Choose yours. Pray this week. And let's get ready to serve our mother through a life-changing week. ❤️

This moment was gold. The kind of pure, grounded love that ties everything together—faith, family, alignment, and the emotional heaviness of what was coming. It wasn't just a sweet text—it was a moment of spiritual leadership from my child, and a beautiful example of what real support looks like when I was facing the unimaginable.

Tears welled up—not from fear this time, but from *being loved.*

Being covered.

Being held.

That kind of love was more healing than any pre-op procedure.

And in that moment, I remembered: I wasn't alone in this.

Not spiritually. Not emotionally. Not even physically.

I had raised children who knew how to call on God… not just for themselves, but for *me.*

And that was the kind of real love I needed going into surgery.

Not pity. Not perfection. Just *presence.*

Then I made another intentional choice: *When I survived* (not if I survived), I would not just recover—I would *redefine.* I would no longer audition for love. I would no longer shrink to fit. I would no longer measure my worth by who stayed, who chose me, or who couldn't. My healing would begin with honoring my value—before anyone else ever had to.

The night before surgery was finally here. Sandra drove down from Richmond with my goddaughter, Nevaeh, who had made it *very* clear she wasn't taking no for an answer about being there. They came with snacks, hugs, and the kind of practical love that makes you feel safe. We laid everything out—hospital forms, appointment instructions, and those awful surgical wipes the doctor insisted I use the night before. I complained the whole time as they made me scrub down like I was prepping for boot camp. The wipes left me sticky and annoyed, but we managed to laugh our way through it. They made sure I followed every step on that"night-before checklist like two aunties who didn't come to play. They joked me about pulling out a cute outfit to wear to the hospital. Nevaeh rolled her eyes and Sandra shook her head, but I reminded them: a lot of things were out of my control—but being cute wasn't one of them. We finished packing. Double-checked the forms. Laughed in between the heavy silences. Then we went into separate rooms, climbed into bed, surrounded by the quiet knowing that tomorrow was coming fast.

Rodney, Miya, and my mom were on the road from North Carolina. Ahkei was in the air from LA. And I was somewhere in between peace and panic, lying in the arms of God, wrapped in the presence of those who loved me.

By 5 AM, we would all be headed to the hospital.

CHAPTER 5

Under the Knife, Into His Hands

We pulled into a mostly empty parking lot. It was too early for most of the world to be awake. The sky was still dark, and the early spring air wrapped around us like a heavy whisper. Rodney and Sandra both drove. I rode with Rodney and Miya, while Nevaeh and Mama hopped in the car with Sandra. Ahkei still wasn't there yet; his flight was scheduled to land around the time I'd be going into the OR. We maneuvered through the lot like a quiet caravan, parking side-by-side, climbing out of our vehicles in slow motion. No one said much. We walked through the chilled air toward the entrance in a single-file line, with me as the line leader, stepping into the unknown. Our footsteps echoed across the pavement, and the silence between us was doing more talking than words ever could. I could sense Miya's mood shifting with every step. Her quiet was louder than usual, and I knew the weight of the moment was sinking in. And although I wanted to shift into "mommy mode and say something motherly and anchoring, this wasn't the moment for any of us to break. So I stayed focused on the tasks: get inside, get checked in, and get ready for what was next. We sat in the registration area—six of us trying to shrink the enormity of the moment into something manageable. It wasn't long before familiar faces began to trickle in.

The first was Kenya.

The moment Miya saw her Auntie Kenya, she cracked. The floodgates opened, and tears poured like they had been waiting for permission. Kenya, true to form, wrapped her up like only she could and let her cry without needing an explanation. At that moment, I knew Miya would be okay. While she cried in Kenya's arms, I sat at the registration window, signing papers, giving consent, confirming emergency contacts, answering questions with a calm voice and trembling hands, and getting all kinds of patient bracelets placed on my arm. After completing the registration process, we moved upstairs to the surgical waiting area. More familiar faces begin to arrive. Intercessors. My First Lady. One by one, they filled the space until we'd taken up an entire side of the waiting room. But they weren't there to spectate. They came to war, shifting the atmosphere. They came to speak to and confront all of the intrusive thoughts and voices of fear that had been speaking to me. Right there in the middle of the hospital's sterile walls, they created a sacred space. Bold prayers. Prophetic declarations. Unshaken faith. They turned that waiting room into a war room. Each of them standing in their anointing, and calling on heaven like they were sure that God would respond.

They circled me, anointed me with oil, laid hands on my head, shoulders, back, and arms. They called heaven down. They didn't tiptoe around the fear—they confronted it. Declaring peace. Declaring healing and declaring divine guidance for every doctor, every incision, every stitch, and stapler. The hospital walls had no choice but to agree with the atmosphere they set. They prayed. I wept. We praised. That floor became holy ground. And as I stood there with the tears of fear releasing from my eyes, I felt carried. Covered. Held. Not just by the hands of those I loved—but also by my Daddy God, the One who loved me first.

As soon as the prayer was over, it was time for me to go to the back. The nurse had come to get me and was patiently waiting until we were done. I hugged everyone. Those were some of the hardest goodbyes I've ever had to walk away from.

As I stepped into the pre-op room, everything started moving fast. Too fast. Gown changes. IVs. Questions. I barely had a moment to think, let alone change my mind if I wanted to. If someone had paused and asked me if I wanted to back out, I swear I would've hit the opt-out button with the quickness; I'm talking no hesitation. Medical staff were constantly coming and going—doctors, nurses, anesthesiologists, and surgeons. Alongside my neurosurgeon, a general surgeon would also be in the operating room to handle part of the procedure. The shunt being placed in my brain required tubing to run down the right side of my neck and into my abdomen, where the excess brain fluid would drain. This meant the general surgeon, whom I hadn't even met until that day, had to make three separate incisions in my stomach to position the tubing properly. I joked with her when she came in to introduce herself, "If you're going to be down there anyway, can I get a little tummy tuck?" Chile...listen, a lot of things were out of my control that day... but being cute wasn't one of them. LOL. But even with the jokes, the weight of it all was pressing down on me. I felt like I was being swept away by a current I couldn't fight.

The anxiety was building. I was overwhelmed—not just by the flurry of medical prep, but by my racing thoughts . How was my family doing in the waiting area? Was Miya okay? Had she stopped crying? And Nevaeh, was she still putting on that brave, nonchalant front she does so well? Would they remember to pick up Ahkei from the airport? And how would he be, knowing he didn't get to see me before I went in? I wondered how my mom and Rodney were holding up, knowing they were listed as my emergency contacts. Were they prepared for the possibility of hearing news they didn't want to hear? As the oldest, Rodney carried a weight that most people don't see. He and I had some hard conversations that I couldn't have with his other siblings. I sent him copies of my life insurance documents. We whispered, and seriously, about a few things that would need to be handled if I didn't make it out. No mother wants to put that kind of responsibility on her child, but he stood there, steady. Holding space. Carrying what needed to be taken. Preparing, just in case.

Just as I was getting lost in those thoughts, I was pulled back into the room by the sharp pricks of needles and the endless stream of questions: "When was the last time you had anything to eat or drink?" "What medications are you currently taking?" "Have you ever had anesthesia before?"

And then…there was the blanket! My nurse placed a warm blanket over me, but it wasn't just any blanket. It was this special contraption, something I'd never seen before. They turned it on, and suddenly, warm air began to flow through it, inflating the blanket like a gentle, heated balloon. It puffed up around me, cocooning my body in this soft, weightless warmth. It felt like being wrapped in a cloud of comfort—like the first real moment of peace I'd had since I'd been taken back there.

For the first time that day, I felt my shoulders drop just a little. My breathing slowed. The tension that had been gripping my chest started to ease. It was such a small thing, but in that sterile, high-stress environment, it felt like a lifeline. That warm, floating blanket became a quiet reminder that I was still here, still grounded, still being cared for.

Once everything was in place, they started letting my family come back one at a time. It was comforting, but it also felt like we were saying final goodbyes all over again. I remember sitting there with my mom, watching her try to take it all in. Her eyes scanned every beep and monitor, trying not to cry as she silently prayed for her baby girl. Then, the curtain opened and another pastor stepped into the room. We didn't even know he was there. He announced that he was strategically waiting for the moment that I was in my room, the moment when we would probably need the reinforcement of more prayer. My mom's face lit up, like God had sent spiritual backup, just in time.

Rodney was the last one to come in. He pulled up a chair beside me, calm and collected. He sat down by the bed and we talked as if we were shooting the breeze, like I wasn't getting ready to go in the operating room to have my skull opened and a device placed in my brain. He had planted himself there like a watchman on duty. Like he had silently agreed to stay with me until the very last possible second, like he understood that at some point soon, I'd be mid-sentence... and then I wouldn't be. It felt like he and the nurse had already had the unspoken conversation, like they both knew what was coming. While I was still suspended in conversation, unaware of how quickly everything was about to change, the nurse approached, quiet and focused, holding the medication for my IV. No words were exchanged. None were needed.

I glanced at Rodney one last time, clinging to the strength in his eyes. The warmth of the air-filled blanket wrapped around me like a soft shield, but even that couldn't hold back what was rising inside me. I could feel the medicine coming through the IV. And then, just like that, I was out.

Out like someone had shut off a light. Out of the moment. Out of my own knowing. Out of my own hands and into His.

While I was under, my family waited.

They prayed.

They paced.

They held their breath through the silence.

The waiting room wasn't just a room that morning—it was a holding place for hope and fear, filled with quiet prayers, whispered questions, and pacing footsteps that tried to outrun the weight of the unknown. Time didn't move normally there. Minutes felt like hours. Every time someone's name was called or a doctor stepped through the double doors, the entire room would shift, shoulders tensed, heads turned, hearts raced.

My family sat in a small cluster, united by a shared heaviness. Miya, already exhausted from holding in so much, had cried herself into a kind of silence that said more than tears ever could. She lay in Sandra's lap listening to *Healing* by Richard Smallwood on repeat in her headphones. Nevaeh slept the time away curled up on a window seat - her body doing what her heart couldn't, which was to rest—her soft breathing representing peace in the middle of chaos. My mom, the quiet intercessor, clutched her purse and her phone; her eyes glued to the doors that led to the operating room, her stare unmoving. As if watching long enough and hard enough could speed up the process or change the outcome.

Ahkei had arrived just in time, strong and full of energy. The life of the party as always - talkin' bout "let's eat." I guess he was hungry from the long flight. He didn't get to see me before surgery, but as a family, they had agreed he would be the first one to see me in recovery. That meant everything to him and me.

Rodney carried the unspoken role of the steady one. He was the one the doctors approached when there were updates. The one the others looked to when they didn't know what to feel or say. He was in and out of naps, not because he wasn't anxious, but because he knew he had to be rested—for himself, and everyone else. Periodically, opening his eyes, scanning the room, making sure everyone was okay, and then resuming the quiet task of holding space for emotions too complex to name.

While they waited, they noticed a man tucked away in the corner of the downstairs lobby, quietly playing the piano. He wasn't performing, just... playing. No introductions, no setlist, no familiar songs, just soft, soul-soothing melodies that floated through the room like a lullaby for their nerves. No one knew what he was playing, but somehow that made it better. There were no lyrics to attach emotions to, no memories stirred. It was just the kind of music that could hush a racing heart and give silence something to rest on.

Miya started calling him *"Piano Guy"*. She didn't know his name, but he became a part of the moment—an anchor in the blur. *Piano Guy* became a core memory of the waiting room, like he was a part of the family. His music wrapped itself around their waiting. Around the pacing. Around the tears that dried and came again. He became their white noise, their steady rhythm during the moments when time felt suspended. It was as if God had sent him to fill the void where words and strength had run out. *Piano Guy* was part of my miracle, too.

Coffee cups sat untouched. Cell phones buzzed occasionally, and when they did, each person looked down quickly, hoping for good news, dreading anything else.

The room itself felt set apart—not because of its décor or function, but because of what it held: faith in action, silent agreements between family members to be strong for one another, and the tension of loving someone who was out of reach but not out of heart. It was where grief tried to take root but was overruled by hope. It was where prayer hovered in the air like oxygen.

I didn't see their tears.

I didn't hear their prayers.

I didn't hold their hands or participate in any of the waiting room chronicles.

I only know what happened out there because they told me. Because they showed me.

The pictures they took. The stories they shared. The moments they remembered.

That's how I pieced it together, how I learned what love looks like in a waiting room.

How I saw what I couldn't see when my eyes were closed.

Their photos became my proof.

Their stories became my memory.

Their presence became my peace.

And knowing now what I couldn't have known while I was under the knife…humbles me. The snapshots of what I never saw gave me a window into the sacrifice they made, not just in showing up, but in carrying the weight of the wait. I wasn't conscious, but they were fully awake, fully aware, and fully committed to loving and serving the person behind the doors. Me. I don't remember the surgery itself, but I remember the love. Because love left evidence in photos and stories. In the way they recalled it, not with resentment, but with reverence.

They informed me that after about 45 minutes into the wait, the general surgeon was the first to come out, letting them know that her part of the procedure, placing the tubing through my abdomen, had gone well. Then they waited some more—eyes glued to the surgical progress boards, whispering prayers with every passing update.

And finally—*finally*—the neurosurgeon came out.

He looked at them and said the words they'd been begging heaven to hear:

"The surgery was successful."

CHAPTER 6

Recovery: The Mirror Could Wait

~

I went into that operating room mentally kicking and silently screaming, but somewhere between anesthesia and awakening, I surrendered. And when I woke up, I was bald on the right side of my head—my hair cut down to the scalp, exposing a fresh horseshoe-shaped incision. Ten surgical staples marked the curve like a zipper, each one holding closed a story I hadn't yet heard. Three more incisions had been made in my stomach to allow the tubing to travel. I hadn't seen any of it yet, but I could feel it. Not just physically—but in my soul.

Waking up in recovery felt like surfacing from the bottom of a deep, dark ocean. I was groggy and disoriented, like someone had unplugged me from one reality and reconnected me in another. The lights were bright. The sounds were muffled. My body felt heavy, foreign—like I was borrowing it for the moment but didn't quite remember how to move it.

Then I heard a familiar voice. "What's up, Dukes?"

It was Ahkei. He's the only one of my kids who calls me "Dukes," which is short for "Ma Dukes." Later, I saw a picture of this moment; he was standing by my bedside, holding my hand, and I was barely awake. I couldn't speak much, my lips barely moved, but I remember trying to smile. I wanted him to know I was still here, still fighting, still me… even if I felt like a different version of myself. And his presence, in that first waking moment, told me that whatever else I didn't know, I wasn't alone.

I had no idea how long I had been under or what updates the family had received. I didn't yet know about the waiting room emotions or the relief that came when the doctor finally told them everything went well and that they could see me in the recovery room. But as I lay there blinking into the blur of recovery, I did know this—I had made it through.

I was still here. God kept me! And someone I loved was sitting right beside me, holding space for my return.

The recovery room is a clouded memory, but my children remembered what I couldn't. Miya talks about how they fed me applesauce, slowly and gently—like I was fragile glass. The nurses told them only two people were allowed in the room at a time, but of course, my three kids had already made up their minds. Rules didn't apply when their mama had just come through brain surgery. They found a way to sneak all three of their bodies into that room at one time. They hovered over me like watchful angels, daring anything—or anyone—to disturb my healing.

Once the initial recovery checks were complete, they wheeled me up to my hospital room, where I'd stay for a day or two. That's when the real planning began. There were whispered conversations about overnight shifts and who would take the first watch. Eventually, everyone went home for a moment to regroup, but Rodney and Ahkei remained. They had a plan to trade off in shifts, but Rodney didn't last long—he crashed in the first hour and went straight to sleep in the corner. I guess he was emotionally drained from the weight of it all. Ahkei stepped into full-blown caregiver mode. For the first six hours in that room, he stayed up, adjusting my pillows, helping me drink water, and making sure the nurses responded when I buzzed. I didn't need to say anything; he just knew exactly what to do. When unfamiliar faces showed up to visit, Ahkei asked without hesitation, "Who are you to my mom?" It wasn't to interrogate. It was to filter. My children were guarding more than my hospital room; they were guarding my healing process. Mama and Miya came back to the hospital later. Mama had made it clear she was taking the overnight shift with me. There's something about a mother's presence, even when you're grown, that makes the room feel more secure.

When all three of my kids were in the room again, the machines began beeping—one of those high-pitched alarms that nurses seem to ignore but family members take personally. It triggered Miya. The sharp, unpredictable sounds sent her back to the trauma of watching her father pass. She tried to keep it together in front of me, but I could sense something shifting in her spirit.

I'm told that it was later, while they were grabbing dinner from Little Caesars, that everything caught up with her. Standing in line for pizza, Miya broke. She cried—hard. She admitted she was terrified of losing another parent. Ahkei comforted her, the way siblings do when there are no words to soothe the moment. They went back to the house and turned on the TV to watch game shows, hoping distraction would mute the emotions from the day. It didn't, but it helped them breathe through the night together.

The kids had also taken my phone. So, back at the hospital, I had no outside voices. No texts, no calls, no pop-up visitors. They had decided that my first night in the hospital was private and that not everyone deserved access to it. Before he left, Ahkei went as far as to print a sign and post it outside my door: *All visitors must check in at the front desk before entering.* It wasn't about being rude. It was about protection. They didn't want anyone walking in to stare at me—bald on the right side of my head, stapled, scarred, vulnerable. I hadn't even seen myself yet. If you were coming into that room, you needed to be coming with love, not curiosity. You needed to carry peace, not pity.

As we moved into the night, Mama became a part of the hospital staff. She used to be a nurse when I was much younger, so she was not playing. She meant business, you hear me. Every nurse who entered my room got the whole Mama scan, a quiet but thorough once-over that made it clear they needed to be on their A-game. She asked questions, watched every move, and made sure no detail in my care slipped through the cracks. She wasn't just my mama, she was my advocate, my eyes, and my shield. She was in Mama bear mode for real.

I was labeled a fall risk. Alarms were strapped to me like silent snitches, tattling every time I dared move or snuck to get out of my bed. I couldn't even pee on my own without setting off a notification. That was the hardest part for me — wanting some dignity and independence but having to rely on someone to escort me to the bathroom. I hated being monitored. I hated needing help to wipe. But I had no choice. This was recovery in its rawest form: humbling, disorienting, and entirely out of my control.

Apple juice and morphine kept me through the night. The nurse eventually came in with a dose of reality: if I kept relying on the morphine, they weren't going to release me to go home. That was all I needed to hear. It was time to thug it out — to breathe through the pain, and deal with it by any means necessary. I didn't want to spend another night in that hospital. I needed the comfort of my own bed, my own pillows, my own peace. Hospital walls, no matter how clean or quiet, could never compare to the healing that happens at home.

The next morning, my neurosurgeon came in for his rounds. All three of my kids were there, along with Mama, posted up and alert. He had this calm, almost playful energy as he walked in. Somewhere along the way, he and Miya had formed a bond—he called her the feisty one, probably because of the way she marched into his office that first day, questions locked and loaded, entirely in protective mode. You could tell he respected her fire by the way he spoke to her first.

He checked in with me, asked how I was feeling, where my pain level was, and how the night had gone. And then came the moment none of us were quite ready for. He said it was time to remove the bandage and check on the scar.

The room fell silent.

We all froze for a millisecond, then quickly tried to gather ourselves. Everyone shifted a little closer to my bedside. I could feel the love tighten around me as tension entered the room. As he started peeling back the layers of gauze, it felt like the whole room was holding its breath. The white bandage stained with blood spots was evidence of the battle my body had just endured. And then he removed it completely, revealing the incision that told the story none of us wanted, but all of us survived. A deep horseshoe-shaped line curved across the right side of my head, held together by ten metal staples. My hair was gone on that side—cut down to the scalp—and in its place was a raw roadmap of what I had just come through. It was jarring. Sobering. Real.

No one said a word at first.

Miya's eyes welled up, her lips pressed together to keep from crying as she quickly looked away. Ahkei, firm in his position to hold me down and nurture me, reached for my hand. Rodney, quiet as ever, gave me a nod like, *You did it, Ma.* Mama stood tall, holding in her nurse instincts and her mother's heart at the same time, but I could see her eyes scanning every inch of the scar, as if mentally assessing the healing already underway.

And me? I couldn't look. I wasn't ready.

I kept my eyes on their faces, watching for reactions and reading the room for signs of how bad it really was. In the most inconspicuous way possible, Rodney quietly took out his phone and snapped a photo, not to post or show anyone else—but to hold for me. For later. For when I was strong enough to see what I had been through.

I knew I had survived, and I was deeply grateful. But my heart couldn't handle the war wounds just yet. Not the visible ones. It was too soon.

After that, things moved quickly. Discharge papers were being discussed, instructions reviewed, and prescriptions written. But my mind was still back at that moment—me, surrounded by my children and my mother, uncovering what I had been too unconscious to witness the day before. It wasn't just a scar. It was a symbol. Of surrender. Of survival. The pain was still present, but so was the strength. It was finally time for me to leave the hospital, and let me tell you, in true retired-nurse-turned-mama-on-a-mission fashion, Mama was packing up like we were restocking a small clinic at home. Toothpaste? Check. Tissues? Check. The styrofoam water pitchers, those little pink basins? Double check. I'm pretty sure we even left with a handful of heart monitor leads—you know, the little sticker things they put on your chest to check your vitals. And then she had the nerve to ask the nurse if we could take the bed props that they had put behind my back and on my side to make me comfortable. Who was telling her no at that point? Nobody. I swear she would have taken the whole hospital bed out of there if we had a way to get it home. SMH…Mama was doing the absolute most! She looked me dead in the eye in front of one of the nurses and said, "You paid for all of this, so we're taking it." And, that we did. Our bags were packed with more than meds. We had a whole *starter kit* for recovery.

I don't remember much of the ride home. I think I dozed off. What I do remember is walking into the house and noticing that all the mirrors had been covered. Towels and sheets were draped gently over the glass. The kids had decided to do that because of my reaction at the hospital when the bandage was removed. They were protecting me from facing too much, too soon. That gesture hit me deep. It warmed my heart in a way that I can't describe. I felt proud that I had raised children with that kind of empathy, that kind of attentiveness. I was incredibly impressed that they would even think to honor the start of my recovery at home this way.

During the first few days at home, I focused on physical healing, knowing full well that I wasn't ready to face the emotional or mental layers just yet. My goal was simple: manage the pain, rest as best I could, and adjust to my new normal, which included figuring out how to sleep without being able to lie on one side comfortably. The day after I came home, the house was packed—Mama, the kids, Sandra, my sister Angie, who had driven in from North Carolina, Nevaeh, and her mom—all circling me with that mix of concern, encouragement, and love that fills a room. Everyone was politely insisting I didn't look *that* bad... until Angie with her unfiltered honesty, walked in and blurted out, "You look terrible." The whole room erupted in laughter. Later, she curled up beside me in bed, and we ate ice cream together, floating for a moment in a sweet, carefree world where nothing else mattered. Then, she tenderly braided the rest of my hair into something that looked more presentable, each twist and turn a quiet act of love and reassurance.

After the first couple of days home, the kids returned to their respective lives—Rodney back to North Carolina, Ahkei to L.A., and Miya to her college campus. Suddenly, the whole house was quiet, and it was just me and Mama. Everything felt like trial and error, wrapped in silent prayers and the steady rhythm of pill schedules. Before I'd left the hospital, they had connected me with an occupational therapist and a physical therapist who began making home visits right away. One afternoon, during a routine check, the physical therapist snapped a photo of my scar for her records. Not knowing I hadn't seen it yet, or that I wasn't ready, she turned the phone toward me and said cheerily, "It's healing nicely—look!"

Mama couldn't stop her fast enough.

My eyes closed on instinct, but it was too late. Even though I didn't *see* the picture, something about the moment shattered my emotional dam. I began bawling and hyperventilating. The therapist was instantly apologetic, her face full of regret, but the impact had already landed. As I struggled to catch my breath, Mama calmly explained to her that I hadn't looked at the scar yet. I didn't have a set timeline for when I would. I just knew I would know when the moment came.

Even though the kids were gone, Mama and I weren't truly alone.

My cousin Kim, who lived nearby, made it her mission to check on me every day. She'd pop in with her bright spirit, plop down in the bed beside me, and keep me company for hours. Sometimes she came bearing desserts—good ones— and one night, she even smuggled in a little glass of wine.

"I promise I won't tell Mama if you give me a sip," I whispered. We were like two little girls in my room, sneaking stuff that we had no business getting into.

She grinned and poured.

Between her quiet joy and Mama's steady presence, my soul found small moments of laughter amid the pain.

And my church, The Mount at Chesapeake. Whew. Deaconess Monique started it when she brought over fried catfish, her infamous Mac & Cheese, twice-baked potatoes, and broccolini (I don't remember much, but Mama and I remember *that* meal). Every evening after that, around 5 p.m., like clockwork, a hot meal was delivered to our door. I was blown away by the consistency, the care, the love. Those dinners felt like love letters wrapped in foil pans. I didn't have the strength to be out among them, but their presence found its way to me.

I didn't know when I'd be ready to see myself fully—not just in the mirror, but in this new life, this post-surgery reality. But what I *did* know was this: healing doesn't rush. And neither would I. Each day, I learned to breathe a little deeper. To trust that the scar I hadn't yet seen was being tended to not just with ointments and gauze, but with laughter in bed from my cousin, hot meals from people who cared, and a mama who knew how to pray and advocate and kids who, from a distance, were committed to loving me to life. The mirrors would wait. My body was doing its part. My soul had begun to stir. I wasn't rushing; I was okay with lingering in that part of my healing because the next step was the hardest: facing myself again.

CHAPTER 7

New Scars that Speak

It took nine days before we removed the towels and sheets from the mirrors.

When the day finally came, I didn't plan it. There was no dramatic buildup, no inspirational music in the background. It was just me, walking past the mirror in my room, catching the faintest glimpse in the corner of my eye... and stopping. I walked over, hesitantly pulling the sheet to the side. At first, my heart hesitated, but then it let me pull just a little more. Before I knew it, the sheet was gone entirely, and the mirror was waiting. I had no problem looking at the three new scars on my stomach. I looked at those every day—lifting my shirt, peeling away little pieces of the glue that held the incisions together, checking the progress like they were tiny badges of survival. But the headshot? That was different. That was the one I had avoided. I knew that one had something to say to my self-esteem.

I took a breath.

Then another.

And then I looked.

What I saw wasn't the horror my imagination had built up. But it wasn't easy, either. The line of staples, the pink angry skin, the places where I thought hair would never grow again—it all spoke louder than I expected. And underneath everything that my eyes were witnessing was the invisible wound to my confidence.

When my new scars started talking, they told a jagged story, one I wasn't quite ready to star in. A story that opened with, *"You've been through hell."* A narrative that told me I was no longer a *normal person* because I was now living with a foreign object in my head. Chronicles that whispered I was somehow less of a woman, with one side of my head bald, bare, and raw. But it was also a story that refused to end there. Its next chapter reminded me that although I had walked through the valley of the shadow of death, I had made it through. My emotions gave mixed reviews on the tales these scars were telling, part trauma, part triumph, and I was the living proof of both.

In that moment, I realized this scar wasn't just evidence of what happened to my head; it was proof of what happened to my soul. I knew then that healing would need to occur in two parts: physically and mentally.

I remember the first day I forgot about the pain in my body and focused only on the ache in my soul. Mama was still with me. That morning, I called my occupational therapist and asked her not to come. I already knew when I opened my eyes that a mental crash was brewing. My heart felt heavy, and the thought of answering questions, getting my vitals taken, or even sitting up to get ready for a visit felt impossible. So I didn't. I stayed in bed.

When Mama realized I'd canceled, concern washed over her face. Still, that wasn't enough to move me. I also decided that answering my phone *is a no-go*—not even for my kids. I wasn't up for the routine *how are you feeling today* questions. Especially not when everything in me wanted to scream, "I feel like absolute sh*t." To make sure I didn't move from that place of bed rotting, I slipped a couple of melatonin pills into my medicine routine, hoping to sleep my way through this mental tsunami.

At some point, Mama walked in holding her phone on speaker. Rodney's voice filled the room, a sharp tone as if he were the parent: "Ma, you need to get up, and if Grandma tells me you took another melatonin, I'm getting on the road and coming there. I'm not playing, Ma, get UP!" I heard him. I let the words land. But still, I didn't move.

By afternoon, I could hear Mama in the other room, talking to people who were checking on me; they had begun calling her phone since I wasn't answering mine. Her voice, filled with so much worry, carried down the hall: "She canceled her appointment, and she won't get up to take a shower." She was talking to my dad, who had been calling regularly to check in, and to my sisters and closest friends who had rallied around. She was talking about me like I wasn't there, and in truth, I wasn't. I had shut down completely…mentally checked out..

The next day, Sandra showed up with my niece in tow. Turns out, Rodney and Mama had called her. It felt like they'd planned an intervention or something. I understood their concern—or maybe I didn't. I value their commitment to not letting me sink too deep into what they saw as a dark space, but I also felt like they should've understood that I needed time to process mentally. It was one day. *One.* Day. (Insert eye roll here.)

Looking back now, I realize that day wasn't weakness—it was a pause. My body had been through trauma, but my heart had been holding just as much. For me, sometimes healing means lying still long enough for the pieces of me to catch up to each other. That pause gave me just enough strength for what came next.

Two days later, I sat on the edge of my bed. My legs felt heavy, my head was tender, but I was upright—and for that moment, upright was enough. Mama peeked in, almost pretending she wasn't checking on me, but I caught the flicker of relief in her eyes. Seeing me on the side of the bed meant I was up and fighting for my healing again.

I wasn't ready to rejoin the world, not yet. But I was prepared to rejoin *myself.* And that started with walking past the mirror again—not to stare or entertain the negative thoughts about my identity, but to nod at the reflection staring back.

The mirrors could wait for the deeper conversation. For now, survival was the story we were telling.

In the days that followed, I focused intently on feeling better and stronger. I was weaning myself off the stronger pain meds, practicing all the life hacks my physical and occupational therapists had been teaching me, and tackling big wins like showering alone and sitting up in the living room for a few minutes to change my scenery.

My oldest sister, Stephanie, was scheduled to pick up Mama soon, which meant I'd need to get used to being mostly alone during this next phase of healing. When Stephanie arrived, I was in such good spirits that, though I was sad she'd be taking Mama back to NC, I was also excited that my sista, the family's hairstylist extraordinaire, was ready to work her hair magic and make me cute again.

Cousin Kim showed up around the same time, carrying some costume jewelry she'd picked up just for the occasion. She was thrilled when I tried on a pair of long, dangling earrings that sparkled like genuine crystals. "It's Dress-Up Dayo Day," she declared.

I slipped those earrings on even before I got my hair done, and boy, you couldn't tell me nothing. I sent pictures to the family group chat with my kids, letting them know that Kim had officially declared it Dress-Up Dayo Day. Our chat lit up.

Ahkei: *"Tell her she's the MVP for the day."*

Miya: *"She slayed the house boots down with dat one."*

Rodney: Heart emojis galore…

Me: *It made me smile A LOT*

The kids were so grateful to Kim for giving me that little glimmer of pretty again. The smile on my face gave them fresh hope that maybe I was getting back to my old self.

Later, Stephanie and Kim went to the store and came back with a wig. My hair was getting washed for the first time since surgery, and it felt incredible to have my big sister's healing hands gently but expertly braiding it down so I could put the wig on. Stephanie had been doing my hair since I was a little girl, and one thing we all know about her in this family is— she can *do* some hair. You hear me?

They had settled on a curly wig for me. We laughed over the stories they shared while trying on and debating which wigs would fit my style best. Kim imagined I'd go for something *big*, while Stephanie was all about keeping it conservative since I had never worn a wig in my life. I wish I could've been a fly on the wall for that debate in the store—lol.

And then the moment arrived: my hair was washed, braided all around the bald area, and it was time for me to put my new hair on. Stephanie slipped the wig on my head, and as soon as I saw myself in the mirror, a little giggle escaped. It wasn't just that the curls were bouncy and full; it was the *newness* of it all. I was looking at a version of myself that I hadn't seen. The version that reminded me that perfection was never a requirement - authentic healing was. There was something about the wig, something about the way it shifted my reflection, that made me feel like I was reclaiming a piece of my identity, even if it was just a small piece. The whole experience, from the wigs to the laughter, was a much-needed breath of fresh air. It reminded me that even in the toughest moments, there's room for joy.

About three weeks into my recovery, I was sitting with a friend. I'd been sharing some of the most personal, unfiltered moments of the brain surgery experience, things I hadn't even told my family, as it related to how I was feeling. And then, almost without thinking, in a voice that was quieter than I meant, laced with something that felt like shame, I said, "I have new scars."

It slipped out before I could catch it, before I could run it through the mental filter that usually keeps my insecurities from showing. Hearing myself say it was like looking in a mirror all over again. This time, vulnerability on a deeper level was staring back at me. It made the tears start all over again.

There was a pause, and then he said, "You are not your scars, and I love you anyway." Something shifted in me right then. That conversation became a defining moment in my recovery. I went away from that conversation, excepting that some scars, old or new, shaped me, but none of them will ever define who I am. It was the moment I realized I had a choice—maybe the only real choice that mattered now. I could decide how much power I gave these marks on my body. I could decide whether they were going to narrate my life or appear in the margins. Because the truth is, scars *do* speak. They tell stories, sometimes in whispers, sometimes in shouts, and sometimes even in shunts. But I didn't have to take every word as truth. I could choose which parts to hear, which parts to mute, which parts to rewrite entirely.

From that point forward, I knew my mental recovery would depend less on what the scars were saying and more on what I chose to listen to. I remembered something my sister Angie once said to my mom years ago: *"Your old friends don't know your new pain."* At the time, I thought I understood her. But now, stitched up and scarred in ways no one could see yet, I felt the weight of her words in a brand-new way. These scars, fresh and unacquainted with my old story, didn't carry the record of every loss, every heartbreak, every fear that had once defined me. They didn't know what I had already survived before life hit me in the head and *57* took over my life, before this incision, before this surrender. And because they didn't know, these new scars were free to tell a different story.

And from here on out, so was I. The old story had its place, its pain, and its lessons. But the new one? This one could hold more grace. More light. More of the kind of courage only found when I stopped fighting the current and let myself be carried into the hands of new transformation. And the beauty of all of this is. I'm not required to reintroduce my scars to my past. They can remain blissfully unaware of all the weight I used to carry. Instead, I get to teach them who I am now and who I am still becoming. I get to decide what they'll symbolize. From here on out, the story is mine to rewrite. I'm not erasing the pain, but reframing it, letting the horseshoe blotch tell a tale of survival, surrender, and the kind of change that isn't handed to me even if I didn't see it coming. I'm speaking to myself and saying, *you have to walk through the fire, bleed for it, and come out the other side with the nerve to call it beautiful.*

My scars weren't done speaking, but now I knew that I would only listen to the parts that would help me shift into the next place of my journey moving forward.

CHAPTER 8

The Shift Beyond the Shunt

~~~

Weeks into recovery, and I knew things were changing. I was physically feeling a little stronger, and I could sense a shift —a quiet, undeniable reminder that God was still masterfully and methodically strategizing every detail of my recovery life.

Remember that job offer I told you about back in Chapter 4? The one that came on the same day I learned I needed brain surgery? Well, let me give you some more details on how that came about and played out in this whole thing.

I'm not sure exactly when I applied for the job, but I remember why. The listing was in Reston, VA, and as a brand-new empty nester after my daughter left for college, I was asking God what was next for me. Was it time to relocate again, to start fresh like I did years ago when I left Richmond for Virginia Beach? I figured if He wanted me to move and do something different in my life, I'd better take some action and start applying for jobs in other cities.

What I didn't know was that I'd be going through the interview process while battling an intracranial pressure of 57, on medical leave, and trying to survive a medication regimen that made it nearly impossible to focus on anything.

The first couple of interviews went well, aside from the usual jitters and nerves. But by the time I got to the later rounds, I was over it. Don't get me wrong, those "You've made it to the next round" emails felt good, but the corporate process — behavioral questions, peer meetings, manager interviews- took energy I didn't have. Some days, it felt like I was dragging my best foot forward through quicksand, hoping it was enough to get me chosen.

By the time the fifth discussion rolled around (not technically an interview, just a chat with the hiring manager), I was ready to throw in the towel. I remember venting to Sandra: *"Girl, they want me to do another interview, and I just can't."* She was patient with me, listening to my frustration before encouraging me to push through. "This isn't an interview; they just want to talk," she said. Then she added something that stopped me in my tracks: *"And when you get done with this one, write your letter of resignation for the other job. Today."*

Wait! Did she know something I didn't? How did she know they just wanted to talk? Why was she telling me to write my resignation that day? Looking back now, that was *God Moment #1.*

I pulled myself together for that final discussion, and Sandra was right. The hiring manager just wanted to connect, answer my questions, and keep it light. Then, in the middle of the conversation, she casually mentioned that the position would now be 100% remote — no relocation to Reston. No commuting to the Norfolk office, as previously discussed, was an option. Just me, working from home, exactly where I needed to be. *God Moment #2.*

After that chat, I sat down and drafted my resignation letter to my current job, without even knowing if I was officially hired. Just like Sandra told me to. *God Moment #3.*

Then, one day while having lunch with Miya, I blurted out a thought: *"If I get this job, I'm going to lose a week of vacation."* The recruiter had explained that the role only came with three weeks of paid time off. On top of that, since the salary range had been based on the cost of living in Reston, I was worried that the shift to remote work might lower the offer. I knew some negotiating was ahead—and let's say I did not have the energy or mental capacity for that either.

Fast-forward to the recruiter's call. I was lying in the chair sulking over the devastating news that I had to have brain surgery when the phone rang. After the greetings, he said, *"We want to offer you the job. And we want to bring you in as a bank officer so you won't lose any of the vacation time you currently have."*

Huh! Say what now? He addressed that first, and I had casually mentioned the concern to Miya. Come on, here' God!

Then he kept going. The salary? Five thousand more than what I'd asked for. Plus, a sign-on bonus. And the start date?

Lined up perfectly—giving me exactly enough time for almost four weeks of recovery and my follow-up visit with the surgeon so I could be cleared for normal activities.

Mind you, this man had no idea about my medical situation. None. Yet the timing could not have been more precise.

God Moments #4, #5, #6—and honestly, by then, I was living in the OVERFLOW.

What I thought was just an application in Reston, VA, turned out to be a divine setup. What looked like an ordinary job opportunity turned into God's way of reminding me that even when I felt weak, confused, or forgotten, He was still in control, strategizing every detail, down to the week, down to the dollar, down to the day.

It was perfect timing, even though it came wrapped in untimely challenges. It wasn't simply a good opportunity; it was a God opportunity. I couldn't shake the feeling that He had orchestrated the timing with divine precision. Instead, He was leading me into something fresh, purposeful, and full of promise.

Preparing for the new job felt like a blur. Somewhere between pre-op panic and prayers, I ended my medical leave, went back to my old job just long enough to hand in the resignation letter I had written weeks earlier, boxed up and mailed back my company equipment, and said goodbye to a place I had worked for twelve years. God was serious about making sure His daughter didn't return to anything that carried the weight of stressful stagnancy. Even now, there are days when I shake my head and say, *"I can't believe I quit a job and started a new one right in the middle of all this surgery mayhem."* But God gave me no time to second-guess, no space to wrestle with the draining emotions that usually come with letting go of the familiar—especially something I had been tied to for so long. I tend to struggle with goodbyes (but that's a whole other issue for an entirely different book).

A couple of weeks into recovery, a bunch of boxes arrived at my front door with the computer equipment for my new job. A friend came over and set up my office while I lay watching this transformation unfold before my eyes. It felt surreal that all of this was happening simultaneously. But here's what God reinforced in me during this time of shifting and healing: two things can be true at the same time. You can be a post-op mess and still stand under an overflow of blessings all at once.

At my follow-up appointment, the doctor gave me the green light to return to work. That clearance brought a swirl of emotions—anticipation, nervousness, gratitude, and a tinge of "Am I ready for this?" This wasn't just about starting a new role; it was stepping into a new chapter of my life. It was about embracing what the shift in the shunt had changed.

The first day was both tiring and amazing. I sat at my desk—with a pillow on standby in case I needed a quick rest—logging into a brand-new world of favor, eager to learn as much as my shunted brain could absorb. To my surprise, I had the absolute best colleague. She welcomed me as if we were family, and it felt like we had known each other forever. Immediately, we bonded as we talked through work responsibilities and what I could expect in this new role. Some people keep work strictly professional, but this connection felt like divine alignment. She had no idea I was fresh out of recovery, yet her daily check-ins and attentiveness made me feel like she was part of another undeniable God-moment.

I remember her saying, *"I can't believe how slow it's been since you started."* She was trying to convince me that it was going to get busier. She even admitted, *"I'm scared at how it has been—it's never been this slow before."*

Those words struck an awareness in me. My first couple of weeks on the job, and in my home office, were part of God moment #… (shucks, I've lost count by now, because at this point God was doing His BIG thang in my life). I wasn't worried at all. I knew it was only slow because God was allowing me more time to heal and recover. He knew I couldn't have started that job at a rigorous pace in the midst of what I was coming off of—so He slowed down the flow.

It reminded me of Psalm 23:2: *"He makes me lie down in green pastures, He leads me beside still waters."* That was precisely what this season felt like—God leading me to still waters, where I could catch my breath and regain strength.

God synchronized my recovery with my new beginning. I was able to start fresh, but in a way that didn't demand more than I could give. Instead of stress, He gave me space. Instead of pressure, He gave me pace. I could sit at my desk, rest my head when I needed to, and let my body adjust while my mind slowly leaned into countless onboarding videos and trainings. It was the best-case scenario of a safe landing (as my Godmother would say) into a new chapter of life.

It was a sho'nuff shift!

There was a time before my surgery, when fear was not a stranger to me. It had been a longtime rival that I worked hard to put in its place. As an empowerment and transformation coach, known as the "fear strategist," I built a significant part of my calling around teaching others how to manage their purpose-driven lives beyond fear. I had helped countless women reframe fear, disarm it, and keep it from taking the driver's seat in their stories. But once I learned I had to have brain surgery (well, actually, when I was diagnosed), fear didn't knock politely; it barged right back into my narrative. It came in uninvited, pulling up a chair and plopping itself down at my table. It disguised itself as caution, responsibility, even wisdom at times, but deep down, it was fear, and for a season, I sat at the table with it and broke bread. I fed off of every story that it had been telling me. It was in the way I packed my hospital bag, wondering if I would ever come home to unpack it. It was in the way I kissed my children, lingering just a second longer because a question haunted me: *What if this is the last kiss they get from me?* It was in the life insurance papers I signed, each stroke of the pen whispering, *prepare them for the worst.* The way I answered the phone the day the recruiter called - fearing rejection. Fear hovered over conversations, seeped into my prayers, and even tried to taint my hope. I entertained its lies and allowed it to remind me of my vulnerabilities.

I was disappointed in myself for letting it set up residency in my head, for entertaining the very thing I had taught so many women to silence. Yet, even in that disappointment, God was doing something; there was a deeper translation of all of the *God moments.* What had once been fear-guided steps began transforming into faith-driven strides. The very shift in my brain paralleled the deeper one happening in my being. But let me be transparent: that shift wasn't as clean and polished as it sounds. As much as I wanted to walk forward in nothing but faith, there were moments I was straddling the faith over fear fence. But with each blessing, each staple in my head, each healing moment, each divine connection, and each manifestation of God's presence, I was determined to embrace the proverbial change of position that my life was taking. It was as if faith had transitioned from a concept I read about in Scripture to a living, breathing reality I could no longer deny. Where I once stayed up at night replaying worst-case scenarios, now I intently rested in the assurance that the same God who carried me through the valley of brain surgery would carry me through the valleys *and* mountains ahead.

The same woman who had once replayed "what ifs" in her mind was now practicing "even ifs." Even if the healing didn't look like I expected, even if the road stretched longer than I wanted, even if tomorrow felt uncertain, my trust in God was growing deeper roots than ever before.

As I reflected on everything: the pain, the fear, the surgery, the recovery, the new job—I realized this wasn't just about what happened in my brain. This was about what was being transformed in my heart and mind. My healing was unfolding. Each day, each step, each prayer carried me further from brokenness and closer to wholeness, and my trust in God was deepening too. What once wavered under the weight of uncertainty was now planted more firmly than it had ever been. My confidence was rising as well. For the first time, I began to believe that there was still a good life waiting for me after brain surgery.

It didn't take long before I shared with my new colleague that I had just had surgery right before starting the job. She sat in awe, her eyes wide, and then said, "You have to tell this story in a book." Little did she know, God had already begun to give me that directive. (Thanks, Cindy, for confirming that assignment!) I knew for sure that what I was walking through wasn't just a collection of scattered God-moments—it was a God-story in the making. Each piece was being written with divine intention, page after page, season after season, all connecting to show me how the hand of God was weaving healing, provision, and alignment into my life. And as I accepted that truth, I also realized something even greater: my God-story could very well become a God-moment for someone else. In the same way, others' testimonies had given me hope. My journey—raw, unpolished, and redeemed- might be the spark that someone else needs to believe the story that God is still writing in their lives, too.

This was the contrast: fear left me drained, paralyzed, and doubtful; faith began to restore me, energize me, and give me a confidence that wasn't rooted in my strength but in God's sovereignty. Pre-surgery, I would have asked, "What if everything falls apart?" The becoming-me, the post-surgery me, began to ask, "What if everything comes together?"

Faith reframed my story, reminding me that God was sovereign, but my response still mattered. What would I do with the life I'd been given back?

CHAPTER 9

It's Up to You Now

W hew! Can I pause here for a second and hold some space for how I'm feeling right now? As I began writing this chapter, I was emotional. I called Miya into my room, and she hugged me as I let out a deep, soulful cry. Reflecting on the journey and writing the previous chapters had been a powerful reminder of God's deep love for me and His faithful care. Secondly, I can hardly believe I'm on Chapter nine of a ten-chapter book that God mandated be written in under 60 days (something I never thought I could do). That fact alone makes my heart swell. I'm proud of my perseverance and overwhelmed with gratitude. The tears rolling down my face as I type the chapter title are the outward evidence of the voice inside me screaming...**THANK YOU, LORD! I'm so grateful.**

Okay, back to our regularly scheduled program.

During my early days of recovery, when my body could do absolutely nothing and rest was my only assignment, I found myself scrolling Netflix in search of something to binge-watch. That's when I stumbled across a show I had never seen before: *The Resident.* Now, this was not my typical kind of show. I usually gravitate toward crime dramas and investigative thrillers, shows like Law & Order and Chicago PD. But *The Resident* was different. It was a full-on medical show. A series centered around a hospital, doctors, nurses, residents... and the messy, life-altering decisions they had to make every single day. Mama couldn't understand why I chose to binge this particular show (and honestly, neither could I at first). After all, it was filled with trauma, medical emergencies, death, and the kinds of scenes that mirrored my fears. Yet, somehow, I couldn't stop. As I watched, I noticed something deeper happening. God was gently showing me that the very things I feared —the medical crises, the uncertainty, the moments when life feels fragile —were reflective recollections of what He had already carried me through. Watching these doctors and nurses navigate crises reminded me that fear doesn't have to dominate my story. I had been given a front-row seat to see resilience, wisdom, and life-saving action in motion, and it felt like a quiet confirmation that I could step back into my own life with courage. The show became more than just entertainment; it became a reflection of a truth I needed to internalize: fear can show up, trauma can appear real and urgent, but God's hand has already been at work, guiding the outcome even when I can't see it. In that sense, the show was almost a spiritual exercise. It allowed me to witness the tension of life-and-death moments, just as I had lived through, but from a safe place. And in that safe place, I could see how I had been changed, how much stronger, more faithful, and more capable I had become. I could face what

I was afraid of without being consumed by it. God was using something that once would have heightened my anxiety to now remind me of my endurance and His sovereignty.

It was here, in this unexpected observation, that the next phase of my recovery began. I understood that while the surgery healed my brain and body, the real work—the choice to trust, to live boldly, and to step into my purpose was mine to claim. The stage was set: God had prepared the path, and now it was up to me to walk it.

Two episodes of the show stood out to me for different reasons, and ironically, both had to do with brain surgery or trauma.

In one episode (Season 5, episode 3), the star nurse, "Nic," was in a car accident and suffered a traumatic brain injury. Her condition deteriorated so quickly that it made my heart race just watching it. The doctors mentioned her *intracranial pressure.* My ears perked up because I knew exactly what that was now. Nic's pressure climbed into the twenties, and the medical team scrambled with a sense of urgency, doing everything possible to get it lower before her brain herniated. Every second mattered. Every number increase meant danger. I remember viewing the monitor on the screen flash the number 22. It wasn't just a statistic in a TV series anymore; it was a number that lived in my body. I knew too well what it meant for pressure to rise, because mine had been a stubborn 57. My chest tightened, my breath caught. If the twenties had every doctor on the show scrambling in a frenzy, then what did it mean that I had been walking around with more than double that? It was as if the weight of what I had endured finally hit me in full.

At first, it was just part of the plot, something for the actors to react to, until it wasn't. I wasn't watching the screenplay anymore; I was watching my near-death truth play out in front of me. That number carried weight. It wasn't just Nic's crisis in a hospital bed; it was my body's testimony. My number had been 57. Fifty-seven. More than double what had the doctors on the screen rushing, calling codes, scrambling to save her. My heart thudded in my chest as I realized: if 22 made for a cliffhanger on television, then my 57 was the real-life miracle.

It was jarring. I couldn't decide whether to keep watching or shut it off. For the actors, it was scripted drama. For me, it was a mirror held up to the unscripted, real life documentary I had lived through; granted, our situations were different with Nic being in a car accident at all, but still. Seeing their frantic response cast new light on my survival, on the skill of my surgeons, the covering of my God, and the prayers that had held me steady. They fought hard, but eventually, their efforts failed. The screen went quiet. The monitors flatlined. And the unthinkable became reality, Nic was brain-dead. The life of that character was over. The moment it hit me, I burst into tears. I wasn't crying just for Nic, a fictional character on a show. I was crying because, for the first time, I truly understood the gravity of what had been happening inside *my head.* It was no longer a medical chart, numbers on a monitor; it was my life and/or death. What looked like punishment in the moment—the shunt, the scar, the surrender to the knife- was my rescue.

Up until then, I had wrestled with this quiet, nagging thought that maybe my surgery had been a punishment, a thorn in my side meant to humble me. I carried questions like, *Why me, Lord?* and *What did I do wrong?* But watching Nic's story play out on screen was like God whispering directly to my spirit: *This wasn't punishment, this was preservation.* What I once perceived as a thorn was His divine intervention to save my life.

That realization broke me open. My tears became a mixture of grief, gratitude, and awe. Grief because I recognized how close I had come to the very line between life and death. Gratitude because God had orchestrated my survival in ways I couldn't even comprehend at the time. And awe because I saw Him not as a distant God dishing out trials, but as a loving Father who stepped in to rescue His daughter.

I started to see it as divine mercy wrapped in surgical gloves and sterile instruments. The hands of the neurosurgeon were the hands of God Himself, steadying the scalpel, orchestrating the timing, and ensuring that I would have the chance to sit here today, writing these very words that you are reading.

It was the transition from *"Why me?"* to humbling muttering of gratitude from my heart and lips, *"Thank You for saving my life, God."*

The second episode (Season 3 Episode 5) that had profound meaning was one where a patient, "Susan," was brought into the hospital after a plane crash. At some point, she had been misdiagnosed with narcolepsy, a sleeping disorder. She had settled into a career that allowed her to babysit her misdiagnosis, jokingly saying to the doctor, *"I travel a lot; at least I can sleep on the planes without anyone questioning it."* Beneath that humor, though, was resignation. She had learned to make peace with *less*, adjusting her whole life to manage what she thought she could not change.

As she told her story, she mentioned how she had seen countless specialists, tried endless medications, and lived under the weight of a diagnosis that seemed to control her entire adulthood. So when the doctors began running new tests, tests that hinted at something different than narcolepsy, she resisted. She was adamant about refusing further treatment. *"I'm sleeping my life away anyway,"* she said flatly. *"And there's no cure for what I have."*

For me, her words immediately brought to mind—and echoed—the story of the woman with the issue of blood, the one who had spent everything she had on physicians, only to find her condition growing worse with each passing day. I could see the same desperation in Susan's voice, the same quiet resignation that comes when every attempt at healing feels like it has failed. She no longer had the strength to fight, to hope, or even to reach for what might save her. And so she said it plainly, with a raw honesty that cut through the room: *"I can't hope anymore."* In that moment, her words were both heartbreaking and profoundly human, a reminder of how physical, emotional, and spiritual exhaustion can silence hope even when the possibility of healing still exists.

But even in her refusal, God left breadcrumbs of what was necessary for healing. As she checked herself out against the doctor's orders, they noticed something small but telling: she was walking differently. That detail suggested a brain issue. They pleaded with her to stay, and this time, she agreed. More tests confirmed a condition that required brain surgery to relieve pressure that had been mistaken for narcolepsy all along.

At the end of the episode, after her surgery, the doctor came to her room for a follow-up. He examined her scar (which was far worse than mine - I'm talking that thing was down the back of her head and into her neck) and told her the successful operation meant she now had the chance at a new life and new experiences.

Their conversation went something like this:

Her: *"This means I don't have to work in sales anymore. I never quit a job before."* (She was genuinely excited about no longer having to settle for a place where she could camouflage her misdiagnosis.)

Him: *"It's up to you now. You've got choices."*

Her: *"Choices. I like the sound of that."*

And in that very moment, I did too.

It was up to me now how I would move on. The doctor's words to Susan—"You've got choices," ricochet in my spirit louder than the monitors that were in my hospital room. I realized that I, too, had choices: I could either take up my sick bed and walk, or I could continue to waddle in what I perceived life had done to me.

The phrase, *"Take up your bed and walk,"* carries such rich weight in Scripture. It is more than just a command; it is a declaration of hope and a call to personal agency. Jesus spoke these words to a man who had been lying in defeat, paralyzed for years, dependent on others for even the smallest assistance. In one simple yet profound statement, Jesus cut through a lifetime of limitation and offered not just healing, but movement, possibility, and a chance at transformation. But the gift was not automatic. It required a decision. The man had to choose whether he would remain on that mat of affliction, resigned to his circumstances, or rise in faith, trusting the One who called him to walk. The choice to move, to trust, to step into the new reminds me that most times, the miracles we long for are intertwined with our willingness to act, to do something, to risk, and to believe that change is possible.

For me, waddling was symbolic of barely moving forward, dragging the remnants of fear, pain, and uncertainty like heavy baggage tied to my ankles. Waddling meant survival, but not thriving. It meant allowing the surgery, the scar, the diagnosis, or even people's pity to define me. Waddling would have kept me safe, but it would have left me stuck, moving in short, halting steps while life and my purpose went forward without me.

But walking was different. Walking meant embracing the fullness of my healing, even if my pace was slow at first. Walking meant trusting God's strength in my weakness, leaning on faith rather than fear. Walking meant leaving behind the bed—the place of sickness, sorrow, and limitation—that had once defined me. Walking meant changing my posture, standing up and living with purpose, not just existing.

And then, if the decision to walk was enough, I remembered a sermon I preached years ago entitled *"I Tread."* The scripture came from Luke 10:19: *"Behold, I give you authority to tread on snakes and scorpions, and over all the power of the enemy."* When I studied the word *"tread,"* I learned it's different from simply walking. Walking can be casual, hesitant, or even distracted. But treading? Treading is deliberate. It's a step that carries weight, authority, and intention. It means pressing down with purpose, asserting not just motion but dominion.

That distinction matters. Because after brain surgery, I didn't feel like treading—I barely felt like walking. I was shuffling, wobbling, waddling through recovery. But spiritually, God was reminding me: you still have authority in your steps. Each shaky stride was more than balance; it was a prophetic act and a determination not to die. My walk was not just about regaining mobility; it was about reclaiming territory. Even if my feet trembled, heaven counted it as treading.

The truth is, waddling requires no courage. Walking requires some effort, but honey, let me tell you… Treading is a whole different layer of courageous action. And courage was precisely what God was pressing into me in that season. Susan's words— *"Choices, I like the sound of that"*—rang in my ears like a personal anthem. I could stay lying in a story of pain, or I could walk into a story of transformation.

And just like that, I realized: waddling was no longer on my list of options. My healing wasn't just survival—it was a commissioning. An invitation to rise, to step with authority, to tread on and crush life's scorpions of fear, anxiety, doubt, and yes, even intracranial hypertension.

I had been given a new job opportunity, but I knew it was only the beginning. Other doors would open, and each one would require me to move outside of my comfort zone. The days of limping through life, dragging my feet in hesitation, or hiding behind medical excuses (even if they were valid excuses) were over.

The surgery had left its mark on my body, but it also left an imprint on my soul: a reminder that I was not a victim of brain surgery, and I would no longer entertain that mindset. I had survived, yes—but more than that, I had been preserved for purpose. It was up to me now to put pressure where the enemy thought I was weak, to plant my steps firmly in faith, and to walk deliberately into destiny. Not casually. Not timidly. But with the sure-footed confidence of someone who knows she has been spared for greater.

From here on, I walk with purpose and tread with confidence—or I don't walk at all.

CHAPTER 10

The Transformation I Didn't See Coming

Today, as I am writing the final chapter, I am exactly one day away from five months since my surgery. I've been to a few follow-up appointments with my neurosurgeon, neurologist, and even my primary care doctor. In addition, I've had a follow-up CT for both my head and abdomen (and they both looked good). I was able to completely come off of the godawful medication(s) that I hated so much and told you about in the beginning (although I'm still on a monthly injection to handle the migraine component that I suffered with before any of this). Most days, I'm symptom-free when it comes to intracranial hypertension, though every so often, the pressure reminds me it's still finding its balance. My doctors told me to expect some bad days while things adjust, and they were right. I've had some of those.

I don't know the exact number of my pressure because that would require another spinal tap, and right now neither I nor the doctors want to put my body through another procedure. They are confident that my condition has decreased from 57, as they are monitoring any symptoms, and the headaches have changed significantly. We will check the actual number at some point, but I agree we should avoid anything else that would require sedation or invasive needles. Right now, kindness to my body looks like allowing it to heal without more trauma.

And my new scars? They are still speaking their own language and telling their story - a story of healing. The angry red lines that once marked my skin have now softened, closed, and faded, leaving behind only gentle reminders of what my body endured and survived. Chile, you should see how hard I'm rubbing that good ol' vitamin E on my stomach every day trying to make sure those blemishes fade. Every scar that has healed feels like a quiet victory, proof that my body is mending and changing in more ways than one.

I am four months into my new job, and I absolutely love it. I enjoy the company and what it stands for, I love my new team, and I'm back to loving the actual work that I do (the last job was chipping away at the passion I had for the actual work). Although I am a remote employee, I travel to one of the headquarters offices in Richmond once a month to work and interact with my team for 2–3 days, which makes me feel like I'm actually a part of something. After five years of working from home and often feeling siloed, that reconnection has been a gift, and I didn't have to relocate to Reston, VA, to get it.

Oh, and my hair! Let me tell you about my hair… first of all, I can no longer see the scar on my head. I can barely even feel it. What once stood out as a painful reminder has now blended back into me—hidden, healed, whole. Over these past months, I watched the back of my head like a hawk, checking it as if it were a progress report from God. I'd place my hand on that spot and rub it often, waiting to see if it felt like life was cultivating black grass again. And it did.

From slick bald to that fresh-shaven look with just a whisper of hair. From the whispers to the stubborn little curly beady beads that reminded me of my African roots. Each new texture was like a testimony sprouting out of my scalp. Transformation in every strand.

I got my hair braided a couple of times, but that little patch at the back, the place where the scar lived, remained untouched. There was nothing there to hold onto. Nothing to grip. Until four days ago, I sat in that braiding chair, and for the first time since surgery, the stylist was able to braid *all* of my hair. Every strand. Every part of me included. That tiny little patch had finally grown long enough to be woven in with the rest. And when she caught it, when she gripped it and braided it, I felt like my whole healing journey was intertwined in that moment too. It may sound small to someone else, but for me, it was monumental. A moment of full-circle celebration. Tears welled up as I said to Miya later that day, "They braided the back of my hair." It wasn't just about hair. It was about scars healed, milestones reached, and the proof that growth comes back even after the most painful cuts.

Technically, I could stop here now that I've given you the most important updates and you're all caught up on my recovery and healing progress. But the truth is, this book was never meant to be a juicy behind-the-scenes read into the gory, emotional details of this season of my life. If it were up to me, I would have continued to heal quietly, privately, holding all those details close to my chest.

But somewhere along this journey of writing, I realized a couple of things:

1. This book *is* a part of my recovery. To leave it unfinished would have been to leave a piece of my healing undone.

2. As a transformation coach, my calling requires me to do more than find transformative lessons in everything; I am called to share them. Because sometimes the very thing we think is *our story* is actually someone else's survival guide.

So here I am, offering up the raw, the vulnerable, the tear-stained, and the triumphant. The true intention of this book has always been to show God that I will stay true to my covenant with Him: to accept my assignment as a wounded healer, and to let you have a transparent look through the lens of the kind of transformation that shows up with no invitation. Because if my scars—now healed and covered with new growth—can point you toward hope, then I know every word, every tear, and every moment of writing this was worth it.

So here goes… let's unpack the transformational lessons that blindsided me, yet ultimately blessed me beyond measure and expanded both my faith and personal growth.

Transformation Is a Trust Journey

A week or so before I went under the knife, I sent a text message to my First Lady at church. She had asked me for some prayer focus points to share with the intercessors. I remember sitting there, phone in hand, heart heavy but steady, and typing these words as *trust* was one of the focus points: *"God and I are on a true trust journey…I don't want to disappoint Him with wavering trust."*

Even as I pressed send, I knew that what I wrote wasn't just a prayer request. It was a confession of where I was and where I longed to be. I was standing in the middle of a storm I never saw coming, and yet something deep within me kept saying, *"If you really believe God is who you've been telling everyone else He is, then this is the moment to prove it."*

Trust sounds so beautiful when we sing about it in hymns or preach about it in sermons. It rolls easily off our tongues when life is stable, when bills are paid, when children are well, when bodies are strong. But trust looks entirely different when you're lying in a hospital bed, doctors preparing to open your head, and you don't know if you'll wake up the same — or at all.

That's when trust stops being a word and becomes a lifeline.

I wasn't asking God for perfect outcomes; I was asking Him for a perfect posture of heart. My greatest fear wasn't death, it was disappointing Him by falling apart in doubt after all the years I had declared His faithfulness. That text message was my way of saying, *"Lord, I'm handing You my trembling hands, my fragile faith, and my whole uncertain future. Please don't let me let go."*

And here's the thing about trust: it doesn't erase fear, it coexists with it. It quietly says, *"Even if I don't understand, I'll lean in to you anyway."* Trust carried me into that operating room. Trust steadied my children when they saw me wheeled away. Trust sat in the waiting room with Rodney. Trust whispered to Miya's fragile heart and allowed Neveah to rest while she waited. And trust stayed at my bedside when I opened my eyes on the other side of the scalpel and saw Ahkei's smiling face.

Transformation, I learned, begins with trust because trust is surrender in action. It's not passive; it's active faith. It's choosing to let God be God, even when every part of you wants to grab control and script the ending yourself. The journey may stretch you, scare you, and surprise you, but one truth remains: you can always, always trust God.

Deal With the Lies Head On

My scars, bald head, and newly implanted devices wanted me to believe that I was broken beyond repair. I struggled with the thought that having a foreign object implanted in my head meant I was no longer *normal.* That robotic comparison crept in, feeding me lies that whispered, *"Your life is over. God can't possibly use you with these kinds of wounds on your record."*

But here's the truth I had to face: lies will always come dressed as facts. They point to the visible, the scars, the changes, the losses, and convince you that what's left is all there will ever be. If I didn't confront those lies directly, they would have written the story of my identity for me. I had to look in the mirror, bald head and all, and remind myself that scars don't disqualify—they testify. Devices in my body don't make me less human; they make me a walking miracle.

It wasn't easy, but I learned to stop agreeing with the lies. I began to speak back to them, to reject shame, and to rewrite the narrative over my own life. Every scar became a reminder of survival. Every device is a marker of God's provision. And every *no longer normal* moment turned into an invitation to embrace a new normal designed by Him.

When you're tempted to believe the lie that you're too broken to be useful, too scarred to be loved, or too altered to be chosen—don't let it sit in silence. Call it out. Name it for what it is. Then replace it with the truth: *I am fearfully and wonderfully made. I am still here. And as long as I'm breathing, God can still use me.*

Heal for You First

When my family would say things like, *"I need you to get better,"* it stirred a question deep in me. One day, I called Sandra and asked, *"Do you think people want you to heal for you—or for them?"*

I wrestled with that thought. Were people anxiously waiting for me to return to normal so I could once again be who I had always been to them? Maybe they were. And maybe that wasn't always selfish, wrong, or nefarious. Of course, my children longed for me to be "Mommy, Ma," or "Dukes" again. Of course, my loved ones wanted their Dayo back. But what I realized in that moment of honesty with Sandra is that if I was going to heal, it had to be *for me first.*

I couldn't just heal to meet the needs of others or to step back into old roles. I had to want healing enough to fight for it— to show up for myself every single day and demand restoration in my own life. Healing had to be a priority, I placed on my own soul before I could be whole enough to give again.

Because true transformation isn't sustainable if it's only driven by the expectations of others. It starts with the courage to say: *I choose to heal for me.* And in choosing that, you ultimately give the best of yourself back to YOU first and then to those who love you.

Accept the Recovery Assignment

I mentioned earlier that this book is a part of my recovery, and to leave it unfinished would have been to leave a piece of my healing undone. The tight deadline for writing this book (under 60 days), combined with editing deadlines and trips down numerous emotional memory lanes, made the whole process feel exceptionally hard. But I learned that if you forfeit the hard assignment, you lose critical pieces of your recovery process, and I was not willing to make that sacrifice. So I buckled down to get it done, sometimes complaining, sometimes getting distracted, and sometimes even trying to calculate an *out* in my head (cause surely I could say this was too much right now), but never giving up on what God required me to do.

There are times in our lives when we ask God for healing, and we must accept that healing His way may come with actions on our part. I am a writer—so naturally, it felt like a part of my healing would come through writing. But if you are on a healing journey of any type in your own life, do the work. Do exactly *what* He tells you to do, the *way* He tells you to do it (it might not be writing a book). Don't sacrifice *complete* healing because the recovery assignment feels hard. When God gives an assignment directly behind or immediately following a low point in your life, don't run from it—show up, do the work, and let your *yes* and obedience be the balm that restores parts of you that prescribed medication can't reach.

And last, but definitely not least… Prepare for the pivotal points of change—even the ones you didn't see coming.

As a coach with a transformation mantra of "Yes! Yes! Yes! Change," I often share a core principle with my clients: walking in your purpose means that you must prepare for the pivotal points of change. *Prepare* doesn't mean you control what happens, but it does mean you expect that life will at times force you to take a hard turn. It's an acknowledgment that life rarely follows a straight and easy line.

I never expected brain surgery to be a part of my story—but it is. I didn't see it coming, yet God used it and continues to use it to build and strengthen me in ways directly relevant to where He is leading me next. Even as hard as it was, I had to choose whether I would bend and grow with these transformative tweaks or completely resist them. Each one, no matter how painful, became a stepping stone that brought me to a place where I can now share my transformation with you from a perspective I never imagined.

Could God have taught me these lessons a different way? Absolutely. But He chose this particular pivot in my life, and I am learning to be satisfied in whatever state He places me. As Philippians 4:11 reminds me, *"I have learned in whatever state I am, to be content."* Contentment here is not passive acceptance, but rather, it's an active choice to embrace the pivotal moments of change, knowing they are shaping me into the person that will accept that greater purpose in my life that He is still grooming me for.

That's it…that's all I got.

I didn't mention you in the acknowledgments, but thank you, my friend. Thank you for allowing me to share my story, for picking up this book and being a part of my recovery journey, and for holding space for me in your heart as you read. Thank you for the prayers you whispered—or even just thought—when you felt the weight of the hard moments in my story, for the moments of empathy, and for believing that I won't stop here. Because you and I both know I won't. I am going to keep growing and trusting God. I am going to keep pursuing greatness and continually connecting my pain points to purpose points. I am going to keep healing, and most of all, I am going to keep embracing transformation. Yes! Yes! Yes! Change!

F It! Reflections

Now that we've walked through this journey together, I want to invite you to linger with me a little longer. Remember earlier in the Author's Note, when I promised you a section of reflections? This is it—our quiet sit-down after all the story has been told. These aren't assignments or homework—although it may be a section to help you apply some of the same resolves to your own change journey. This is simply a space for you to dive deeper into some my raw emotions, breathe, and process what you've just experienced alongside me.

Each "F It" Reflection is how I faced it, felt it, faithed it, and finally found my way through it. I moved through three simple lenses:

- **Fear Acknowledgement** – naming the real, raw fears that show up when life turns upside down.
- **Faith Reflection** – leaning into scripture and letting God's truth speak louder than the pain.
- **Final Resolution** – anchoring yourself in hope and transformation as you take the next step forward.

Take your time, let your heart respond, and allow these reflections to meet you exactly where you are if by chance you are learning to face, feel and apply faith in a very hard season. Think of it as our conversation, one-on-one, after the storm — a chance to process, release, and lean into hope and transformation together, without pressure, judgment, or expectation

Chapter 1: When Life Hit Me in the Head

Fear Acknowledgement

I was afraid of what I couldn't name.

Afraid that the pain shooting through my body was more than stress, more than fatigue.

Afraid that I was losing control of the one thing I had always been able to push through—myself.

Life was coming for my head—not just physically, but spiritually and emotionally. Yes, the headaches were unbearable, my vision was distorted, and my life felt unsteady. But deeper than the symptoms, I sensed that my purpose was under attack.

The head is where thoughts form, where dreams take shape, where vision is cast, and clarity is born. And mine felt like it was unraveling. I feared I was losing more than my health—I feared I was losing *me*. Who would I be if I couldn't think clearly, write freely, or function at full capacity? Would I be forced to surrender to a life defined by illness? The fear wasn't only about dying—it was about slowly fading out of the purpose I had spent years stepping into.

Faith Reflection

But even in the fog, God whispered. Steady. Gentle. Faithful.

He reminded me that He is the keeper of my mind and the Author of my story. That even when my thoughts slipped, when my peace wavered, when my clarity vanished—He was still holding the pen.

I anchored myself in a scripture that had carried me through countless storms:

"Being confident of this very thing, that He who began a good work in you will carry it on to completion until the day of Christ Jesus." — Philippians 1:6

This wasn't the end of me. It was the continuation of a good work—one that He Himself started. And if God begins it, He always has a plan to finish it.

Final Resolution - To Believe Anyway

I chose to believe that God was not finished with my mind—or my mission.

That even in the unraveling, He was weaving something deeper.

That His hands were on my head—not just steadying pressure points, but safeguarding my calling, my creativity, my clarity.

So I surrendered. I said yes to transformation. Not the polished kind, but the raw kind—the kind that begins when your world caves in and your soul decides to keep believing anyway.

Chapter 2: Fifty Seven: Does Pressure Really Bust Pipes

Fear Acknowledgement

I was hurting—deeply, physically, and emotionally. I was afraid of the pressure pressing in on every side and of being left alone with my pain. I thought something might happen while I was by myself. The thought of slipping into a medical emergency with no one around haunted me.

I feared the unknown side effects, the silence, the weight of isolation. But beneath all of that was a deeper fear—that this might never get better. That I would be trapped in this version of my body and mind forever.

Faith Reflection

When I packed my bag and drove five hours to Mama's house, I wasn't just escaping fear—I was running toward a place saturated with prayer and love. Mama, a bona fide intercessor, had oil-stained hands and war-room words that I knew could help carry me when I couldn't carry myself.

I anchored myself in Psalm 91:4-5:

"He will cover you with His feathers, and under His wings you will find refuge; His faithful promises are your armor and protection. Do not be afraid of the terrors of the night, nor the arrow that flies by day."

I wasn't abandoned. I was cradled—in discomfort, yes—but also in divine protection. God had already promised He would shield me, even from deadly disease.

Final Resolution - To Rest Under His Wings

So, I stayed. Not just in my mother's house, but in the posture of allowing others to care for me… and letting God redefine what strength really meant.

I didn't need to prove my faith by pushing through alone. I could trust Him in the resting, in the wrestling, and in the waiting.

I released the lie that stillness meant weakness—and began to embrace it instead as holy ground. A place where transformation could quietly take root under the shelter of His wings.

Chapter 3: Oh Sh...Shunt!

Fear Acknowledgement

I was afraid of surrendering control. Afraid of what brain surgery would mean for my future, for my identity, for my ability to function. I feared being cut open, the unknowns of recovery, and everything that could go wrong.

But beneath all of that, I wrestled with a deeper torment—the reality that I couldn't fix this on my own. I had tried everything—rest, remedies, an abundance of stupid medications, prayer, sheer willpower—and nothing worked. The feelings of helplessness scared me and made me feel like I had failed at holding my own life together.

And then came the part I was almost too ashamed but also bold enough to admit: I feared becoming angry with God. Angry that He had brought me to this place where all my strength, all the medications, all my faith practices still led me here—facing surgery. It felt like being backed into a corner, I couldn't pray or push my way out of. I worried that if I gave voice to that anger, I'd somehow forfeit the very faith I had built my life on.

So my fear wasn't just about scalpels and outcomes—it was about unraveling inside. About losing not only control of my body, but also the trust I had always clung to in God.

119

Faith Reflection

Somewhere between my daughter's tears and the surgeon's steady confidence, God broke through my spiraling thoughts. Not with rebuke, but with reassurance. I felt Him whisper: *"I see you. I've always seen you. This has never been out of My hands."*

And in that moment, I realized something important: God wasn't offended by my wrestle. He could handle my honesty, my questions, even my brewing anger. His love wasn't fragile. His promises weren't voided by my doubts.

Isaiah 41:10 became my place of reason:

"Fear not, for I am with you; be not dismayed, for I am your God. I will strengthen you and help you; I will uphold you with my righteous right hand."

This wasn't punishment. It wasn't abandonment. It wasn't God turning His back on me. It was Him holding me steady—even when I struggled to hold on to Him. This was part of a plan I didn't choose, but one I was slowly learning to trust.

Final Resolution — To Embrace the "Oh Sh...Shunt" Moment

I said yes—again. Not just to surgery, not to suffering, but to God. I gave up my control and placed my life in His hands.

I chose to believe that even this could be used for my good and His glory. I surrendered my plan and leaned into the One holding the master blueprint. This wasn't the transformation I imagined, but it was the one tailor-made for my healing.

Chapter 4: Pre-op Panic & Prayers

Fear Acknowledgement:

I was terrified.

Terrified of the unknown.

Terrified of the operating room.

Terrified of never waking up.

There were nights I lay still, haunted by intrusive thoughts I couldn't pray away. I feared being declared brain-dead. I feared dying before getting to truly live. And more than anything, I feared leaving my children behind—mid-conversation, mid-miracle, mid-story.

It wasn't just about my physical head... it was about what my head held: dreams, vision, purpose. Everything I'd been birthing in others, I feared I might not live to see fully born in me.

Faith Reflection:

"Three times I pleaded with the Lord to take it away from me. But He said to me, 'My grace is sufficient for you, for My power is made perfect in weakness.'" — *2 Corinthians 12:8–9*

Like Paul, I begged.

"Take this thorn, Jesus."

I thought I had already done enough to be healed.

I'd served, I'd prayed, I'd surrendered. So why was this still mine to carry?

But when the thorn didn't move, His grace did.

It wrapped itself around my panic like a weighted blanket, reminding me that I wasn't being punished—I was being held. His grace was sufficient... not in theory, but in practice.

Not in the absence of fear, but in the presence of it.

Final Resolution — To Accept the Thorn

I couldn't remove the thorn. But I could release my grip on the fears that had been plaguing my thoughts.

I chose to trust. Trust through the sting of those pre-op wipes. Trust through the mix of laughter and tears with Nevaeh and Sandra. Trust, even as I packed my hospital bag and slipped in a cute outfit, God's grace was saturating my life even in my weakness.

I made a decision: I will not die the way I once lived— shrinking, unsure of love, bending to fit in. If I'm going to walk through this valley, I will walk with grace, with grit, and surrounded by the people who truly love me. And most of all, I will walk with God. Thorn and all, I am not walking alone.

Chapter 5: Under the Knife and Into His Hands

Fear Acknowledgement

This was it. No more postponing, no more rehearsing the "what ifs." I was about to be put to sleep, with no guarantee I'd wake up the same, if at all.

The thought of anesthesia pulling me under felt like handing my very breath to strangers. I feared not waking up. I feared waking up different. And somewhere deep inside, I feared waking up to a life I no longer recognized.

Faith Reflection

"When I am afraid, I put my trust in You." — Psalm 56:3

I had done all I could. Prayed all the prayers. Hugged all the necks. Said the hard goodbyes, just in case. But there comes a point where faith has to stop talking and start resting.

So in that sterile room, with bright lights above me and fear swirling inside me, I shifted my focus. I remembered the God who first breathed life into me, the One who knit me together before a surgeon ever held a scalpel.

As my eyelids grew heavy, I whispered, "Lord, I'm Yours." I wasn't surrendering to medicine—I was surrendering to the One who created medicine. My body might be under their hands, but my life was in His.

Final Resolution — To Release Control

So, "F it" (face it, feel it, faith it) —I let go.

I let go of the need to know how it would all play out. I handed God my pulse, my breath, my future.

And as the room faded, I didn't fight it. I rested. Because faith isn't just believing God *can*—it's trusting Him when you're unconscious and can't do a single thing or see *how* He's doing it.

When I woke up, I knew something had shifted. Not just in my head, but in my heart. Fear no longer had the final say. From that point on, my "yes" to God wasn't timid or conditional—it was whole.

I walked out of that valley of the shadow of death with a scar, yes—but also with proof. Proof that surrender isn't weakness. Proof that God's hands really do hold what ours can't. Proof that even when I'm cut open, He is still writing healing into my story.

Chapter 6: Recovery- The Mirror Could Wait

Fear Acknowledgement

I was scared to see myself.

Not the version in the hospital gown—that part was expected. What terrified me was meeting the "after" me. The one marked, stapled, and stitched together. The one whose reflection might remind me more of what I'd lost than of what I'd survived.

The thought of facing that mirror made my chest tighten. I knew the physical wound would heal… but would my soul recover?

Faith Reflection

"He heals the brokenhearted and binds up their wounds." — Psalm 147:3

Healing wasn't only in the surgeon's hands—it was in God's. He wasn't just binding my head—He was binding my heart. And until I was ready to face myself in the mirror, He surrounded me with the faces of my children, my mother, my sister, my cousins, my church family.

They became my reflection. They showed me strength when I couldn't see it in myself.

Final Resolution — To Heal on My Terms

So I decided I wouldn't rush. The towels would stay on the mirrors until I said otherwise. The scar would reveal itself when my heart was strong enough to bear it.

In the meantime, I let love do its work—through Mama's watchful care, Cousin Kim's desserts, the church's meals, even the stolen sip of wine.

Because sometimes "F it" doesn't mean charging forward. Sometimes it means granting yourself permission to heal slowly, fully, and without apology.

Chapter 7: New Scars That Speak

Fear Acknowledgement

The first time I caught my reflection after surgery, I barely recognized the woman staring back. The swelling had gone down some, but the scar still curved along my head like an uninvited signature. And then there was the wig—smooth, styled, and perfectly placed—yet it whispered a story I wasn't sure I wanted to tell. I feared that anyone who saw me would see the wig first, then try to piece together the "why." My mind ran ahead of me, creating narratives that weren't mine but that I felt obligated to explain. It was the fear of being defined by the evidence of my survival rather than the essence of who I was.

Faith Reflection

But then I remembered: God has always had the final word on my identity. I thought about the scripture that says, "*You are altogether beautiful, my darling; there is no flaw in you*" (Song of Solomon 4:7, NIV). My worth wasn't hidden under hair or exposed by its absence. The wig wasn't a mask—it was a covering for this season, no different than the way God covers me with grace when my wounds are still healing. If He could see me as whole, even with fresh scars, then I could learn to see myself the same way.

Final Resolution - To Decide What Speaks to Me & How I Speak Back

I'm not going to let the mirror dictate my mood, my confidence, or my testimony. I'll wear the wig without apology and, when I'm ready, I'll wear my natural hair without shame. My story doesn't start or end at my hairline. My reflection is more than the surface—it's the resilience in my eyes, the gratitude in my smile, and the unwavering truth that I am still here. And that is beautiful.

Chapter 8: The Shift Beyond the Shunt

Fear Acknowledgement

At first, I feared that the surgery would leave me broken beyond repair—not just in my body, but in my spirit. I worried that the woman I used to be had been left on that operating table, and that the version of me who survived wouldn't be enough to carry on with purpose.

Faith Reflection

But God was faithful in more ways than I could count. He was not just healing my brain—He was renewing my being. Just as Psalm 23:2 reminds me, *"He makes me lie down in green pastures, He leads me beside still waters."* God slowed me down, not to punish me, but to restore me. In the stillness, I discovered that my trust in Him deepened. My faith was no longer surface-level; it was rooted in the truth that He had kept me alive with intention.

Final Resolution - To Shift with the Shunt

This was more than a medical recovery. It was a **major shift**—in my healing, in my confidence, and in my relationship with God. My body was learning how to function again, but my soul was learning how to flourish. I started to believe that there was still a *good life after brain surgery.* A life where healing and hope could coexist. A life where confidence was rebuilt, not on my own strength, but on the One who had brought me through. My brain had shifted, yes—but so had my being. And in that shift, I found new life.

Chapter 9: It's Up to You Now

Fear Acknowledgment

The hardest part of healing is realizing no one else can make the choice for me. Doctors, family, and friends could support me, but ultimately, I had to decide whether I would live in fear of what happened or step into faith for what's ahead. The fear whispered: *What if I choose wrong? What if I'm not strong enough to carry this new version of myself?*

Faith Reflection

Joshua 24:15 says, *"Choose this day whom you will serve."* Life after surgery left me at a crossroads. My choice was not just about survival—it was about alignment. I had to decide if I would serve fear or faith, defeat or destiny, pain or purpose. The reminder was clear: God entrusted me with choice, and choosing Him meant choosing life.

Final Resolution: To Make the Right Choice

I chose forward. I chose healing. I chose life. Even with uncertainty still present, I declared with my choice that I would not stay stuck in fear. My scars became my evidence that God had already carried me through the worst, and my decision to keep moving became my testimony that healing is a daily, deliberate choice.

Chapter 10: The Transformation I Didn't See Coming

Fear Acknowledgement

I was afraid that the new version of me—bald head, healing wounds, implanted shunt—wouldn't be enough. I feared people would compare me to who I once was and decide I no longer measured up.

Faith Reflection

But God whispered to me that transformation always reshapes us, inside and out. The external changes may feel jarring, but His hand is still at work molding me into who He always intended me to be. *"Being confident of this very thing, that He who hath begun a good work in you will perform it until the day of Jesus Christ"* (Philippians 1:6). My identity isn't wrapped in hair, skin, or medical devices—it's anchored in Him, and He has promised to finish the good work He began.

Final Resolution — To Say "F IT" to Everything & Transform

"F it" to the fear of no longer being enough. I release the doubts, the what-ifs, the comparisons that once held me hostage. I choose instead to embrace the transformation I never saw coming—the kind that arrives through pain, uncertainty, and surrender.

Scars, shunt, and all, I am saying yes. Yes, to the process I didn't plan. Yes to the growth I didn't expect. Yes, to the woman God is shaping me to be. I trust that every stitch, every procedure, every moment of vulnerability is part of a divine design, ushering me into my next season with strength, clarity, and purpose.

I am learning that transformation isn't always tidy or comfortable. It's raw. It's persistent. It demands patience and courage. And yet, it is beautiful—because it's mine, and it is orchestrated by the One who sees the beginning, the middle, and the end of my story.

I step forward fully, without apology, fully alive in the unfolding of His plan. This is my transformation. This is my declaration: I am enough. Whole. Resilient. And moving boldly into the woman I am meant to become.

Returning to Give Thanks

~

As this journey closes in the pages of this book, I feel the need to write back—to respond, to reflect, and to tie up the loose threads of my heart with Yours.

God, You were the only one who could be considered the subject matter expert in my life—the only one whose words could set the stage for what was to be shared in this book. You spoke to me straight from Your heart, reminding me of Your love, Your plan, and Your perfect timing. I write back in response to what You shared in the foreword—not as a question, not as a plea, but as Your daughter who has seen, felt, and grown through it all.

Now, here I am, like the one leper in Luke 17:11-19 who returned to give thanks after being healed, I am coming back to You, heart full, to say thank You. Thank You for the storms I could not see past, for the silence that felt too long, and for the lessons that cut deep. Thank You for shaping me, refining me, and carrying me even when I didn't understand. I see now that everything You allowed, everything You placed in my path, and even the shunt that was placed in my head, was for my good.

I want You to know—I am no longer angry. I am no longer questioning Your heart. I trust You. I trust Your timing. I trust that every tear, every trial, and every triumph was meant to draw me closer to You. Our covenant stands, unshaken. I am Yours, fully. I am grateful. I am healed.

From the heart of Your daughter,

—Me

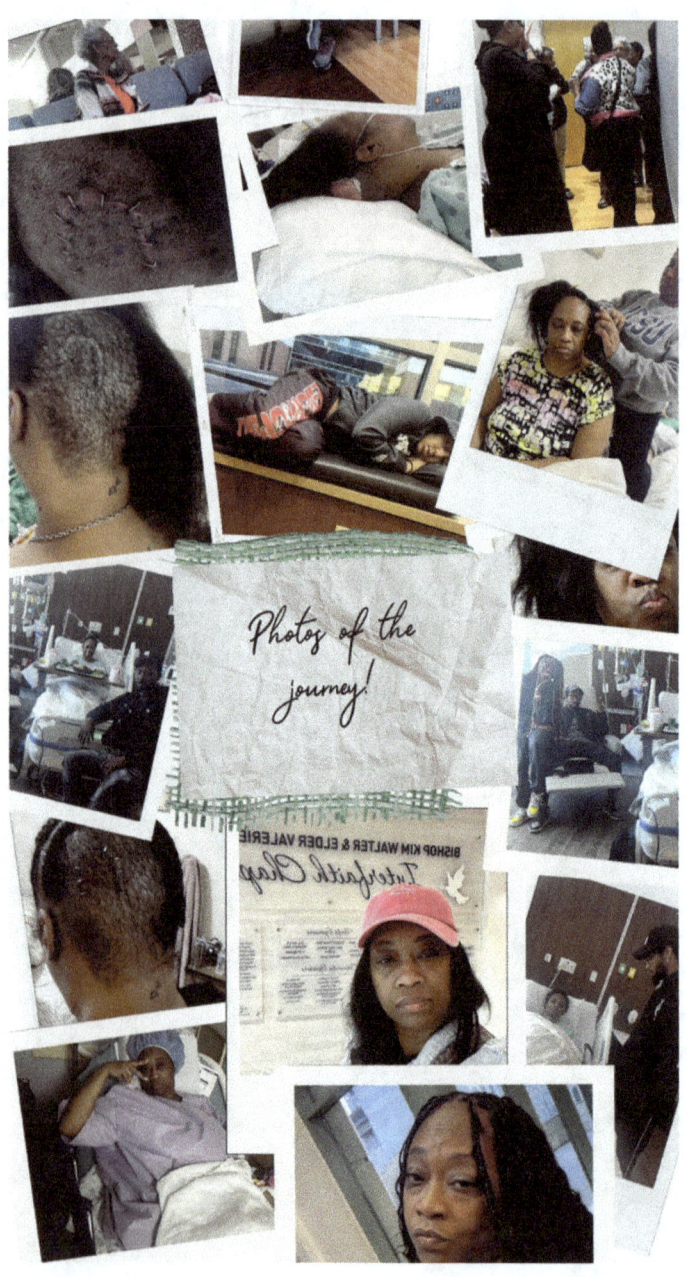

Photos of the journey!

www.ingramcontent.com/pod-product-compliance
Lightning Source LLC
Chambersburg PA
CBHW071310130626
46556CB00004B/1551